Find Out About PRAYER

Charles E. Bradford

HART RESEARCH CENTER
FALLBROOK, CALIFORNIA

Edited by Ken McFarland
Cover art direction and design by Ed Guthero
Cover illustration by Nathan Greene

ISBN: 1-878046-20-9

Contents

Seeking His Spirit
for Service
Prayer Works!

Preface

More and more, church members across North America are reaching out after God and spiritual things. People want to know God for themselves. They are not interested in nice books and articles about Him—they hunger and thirst instead for His actual presence. No, as yet it is not a mass movement or a great public demonstration, but if not spectacular or dramatic or sensational, it is nonetheless real.

In growing numbers, church members are not willing to wait for the crowd. In Seventh-day Adventist communities large and small, in great institutional settings and out of the way places, and without any central planning or prodding by official committees, the people of God are "moving into line." Prayer circles, small-group ministries, prayer warrior bands, conferences on prayer and spirituality, and koinonia (fellowship) cells can be found in conference offices, dormitories, classrooms, and committee rooms.

Some do not sense what is happening—what a pity.

"He who has an ear, let him hear what the Spirit says to the churches." Some of our New Testament scholars say there is a case for translating the text to read "He who has an ear, let him hear what the Spirit is saying *among* the churches."

It is possible to be in the midst of a spiritual awakening and be unaware of it—to be ignorant of what the Spirit is trying to tell us. Even while the latter rain is falling, a great many "saints" will not know it is happening. "Earth's crammed with heaven," the poet said, "and every common bush afire with God; but only he who sees takes off his shoes, the rest sit around and pluck the blackberries."

A veteran pastor who had written several deeply spiritual books and effective Bible correspondence courses paid me a visit one day. He wanted me to look at his latest manuscript. One of the illustrations he used caught my eye. It was about a tall-masted sailing ship that some entrepreneurial spirit brought to the Niagara River. It proved to be a great attraction. Crowds thronged both banks to see it.

Then came a day when the tow rope broke. The big vessel was now near the falls. A feeling of hopelessness seized both passengers and spectators on the riverbanks as the ship drifted ever nearer the point of no return. Then the captain gave an unusual order. "Hoist every sail," he shouted through the megaphone. "Every piece of canvas in the air!" He had felt the gentlest of breezes and believed the wind would pick up—and it did.

After an agonizing, almost unbearable moment, the sails began to take wind. Soon they were billowing. The big craft slowed till it was dead still, then gradually began to reverse course. The reaction was overwhelming. People shouted, cried, whistled, and stomped their feet. Men threw their caps in the air; women waved their handkerchiefs wildly. "She's saved! She's saved!" the shout went up on both sides of the Niagara.

The most spiritual people I know report that a gentle breeze is ablowing. It may be just a zephyr now, but soon it will become a gale, and in God's own time a mighty wind, earthshaking and awesome. Isn't it about time we threw up every sail, every piece of canvas, and made every effort to be in the line of the rising current? We cannot produce the wind, but we can hoist our sails. We can open our souls heavenward to catch the wind. There *is* something we can do.

So I join with my spiritually sensitive brothers and sisters who are turning toward heaven in earnest, persistent prayer. We have every reason to believe that the mighty winds of Pentecost will blow upon us, because Christ has promised it. "Floods of spiritual power are to be poured forth upon those prepared to receive it"—*Testimonies,* vol. 8, p. 46.

This little book goes out in support of the call to prayer that the Holy Spirit has moved our leaders to sound throughout North America.

"Open my eyes, that I may see,
Glimpses of truth You have for me;
Place in my hands the wonderful key
That shall unlock and set me free.

"Silently now I wait for You,
Ready my God Your will to do;
Open my eyes, illumine me,
Spirit divine!"
—Clara H. Scott

We want to see a genuine spiritual awakening in North America, but we know full well that revivals are not worked up, they are prayed down. So come, my sisters and brothers, join me in fastening all our powers with laser-like intensity on the communication system through which all the vast treasures and riches in glory come to us.

The call coming to us today is a call to focus on prayer.

Charles E. Bradford
January 1993

Foreword

With the *Titanic* going down, there are better things to do than rearrange chairs on the deck. And when the house is on fire, dusting the furniture can't be the best use of time.

Emergencies resort our priorities—or should.

And when it comes to what our priorities should be as a church, we certainly have not been left in doubt:

> "A revival of true godliness among us is the greatest and most urgent of all our needs. To seek this should be our first work."—*Selected Messages,* book one, p. 121.

Greatest . . . most urgent . . . first. Priority One.

Looking back, we see what can happen when God's people are revived. Pentecost unleashed a torrent of spiritual power that swept thousands into the Kingdom of heaven and must have left the prince of darkness badly shaken.

And looking forward, we yearn for the arrival of earth's last and most powerful revival—Pentecost II:

> "Before the final visitation of God's judgments upon the earth there will be among the people of the Lord such a revival of primitive godliness as has not been witnessed since apostolic times."—*The Great Controversy,* p. 464.

In between these two mighty revivals, the church has seen others: the Reformation, the second-advent awakening of the 1840s, to cite examples.

One unassailable fact emerges from any careful focus on revivals, past or future: *every revival that has ever happened—or that ever will—has been (and will be) touched off by prayer!*

We must return to book one of *Selected Messages* and read just a few more lines:

> "A revival of true godliness among us is the greatest and most urgent of all our needs. To seek this should be our first work. There must be earnest effort to obtain the blessing of the Lord, not because God is not willing to bestow His blessing upon us, but because we are unprepared to receive it. Our heavenly Father is more willing to give His Holy Spirit to them that ask Him, than are earthly parents to give good gifts to their children. But it is our work, by confession, humiliation, repentance, and *earnest prayer,* to fulfill the conditions upon which God has promised to grant us His blessing. *A revival need be expected only in answer to prayer.*"—page 121, emphasis supplied.

Revival is priority one. And prayer is what brings it. Prayer is the match that touches off the spiritual explosion.

The Seventh-day Adventist Church may be hurtling, along with everyone else, toward A.D. 2000. But for many of us, the perception is that somehow we've stalled on the way to rendezvous with our returning King.

And here in North America where the advent revival was born, growing numbers of members and church leaders long for the last great awakening of God's people. As the years and decades pass, the prospect of "business as usual" has become utterly intolerable. The world cries out in its great need for what only a revived church can offer. It is time and past time for something extraordinary—something earthshaking—to happen. "And when they had prayed, the place was shaken . . ." (Acts 4:31).

Do we desperately need to be roused, revived, shaken? Then we must pray. We must pray as we have never yet prayed. We must pray one by one—seeking God for Himself alone and not just for what He can give us. We must pray in order to know Him, whom to know is our eternal life.

And we must pray together. We must become the church on its knees, seeking His presence, His power, His gift of unity with a determination that will not be denied.

It is time for prayer with a purpose—prayer that seeks the Holy Spirit for power in service—prayer that seeks the expulsion of personal and corporate selfishness so that in us the world sees only Jesus.

Recently the leaders of God's work here in North America met to discuss priorities for the church in this division. Out of those prayerful deliberations emerged the conviction that a new and unprecedented call to prayer is needed—that an appeal must go forth to every member in this field to turn from life's frenzied pursuits and even television's mesmerizing images to seek God—as never before—on our knees.

As a part of this urgent new call to prayer, Elder Charles E. Bradford has written this book. Elder Bradford's leadership in North America and throughout the world has been marked by his emphasis on the Word of God and prayer. And in the pages ahead, he focuses without deviation on the practice and priority of prayer.

If prayer is in fact the match that touches off revival, we must find out about prayer. If prayer is the key that unlocks heaven's storehouse, we must find out about prayer. If only prayer will unleash the awesome power of the Holy Spirit, we simply *must* find out about prayer.

"Lord . . . *please* . . . teach us to pray."

A.C. McClure
President, North American Division of
Seventh-day Adventists

1

Find Out About Prayer

"We must turn away from a thousand topics that invite our attention. There are matters that consume time and arouse inquiry, but end in nothing. The highest interests demand the close attention and energy that are too often given to comparatively insignificant things"
—*Testimonies,* vol. 8, p. 316.

Find out about prayer! Someone must find out about prayer!" Albert Einstein is reported to have said to his staff as he approached the end of his long and distinguished career. Perhaps the great scientist was thinking about researching the subject. That's the way he would have addressed a problem. He had spent a lifetime observing the laws that govern the universe. But this man who did more than any other scientist to unlock the terrible secrets of the atom, who one day went to the chalkboard and wrote $E=MC^2$—the equation that changed the world forever—wanted desperately, as he neared the end of his life, to discover the dynamics of prayer.

If we are going to meet heaven's expectation for us as we approach the third millenium and time's end, we shall have to find out much more about prayer. If we are to unlock the secrets of personal growth in grace and release the enormous power God has made available to His church for the accomplishment of His purposes in the earth, we shall have to get serious about the science of prayer. We need to find out about prayer. It's crucial.

One of Professor Einstein's contemporaries, Alexis Carrel—himself a world-class scientist—put it this way:

> "Prayer is the most powerful form of energy one can generate. The influence of prayer on the human mind and body is as demonstrable as that of the secreting glands. Prayer is a force as real as terrestrial gravity. It supplies us with a flow of sustaining power in our lives."—Frank S. Mead, *The Encyclopedia of Religious Quotations,* Revell.

The Place to Begin

Where shall we begin? To be sure, with ourselves. Our own need is the foremost consideration. To see ourselves as we really are—as we actually appear before God—will drive us to our knees. I am not talking about an obsession with morbid introspection, or excessive brooding, or endless self-analysis, as if we could ever fully know ourselves. I am talking about submitting to the examination of the Great Physician. It is dangerous to rely only on self examination. "Search me, O God, and know my heart" was David's prayer (Psalm 139:21). He knew from bitter experience the danger of relying solely on self examination. We must look to a Power out of and beyond ourselves, or we will make a disappointing false start.

The problem with the Pharisee in Jesus' parable was

that he never saw himself as he really was. Ellen White describes the predicament: "His soul was encased in an armor of self-righteousness which the arrows of God, barbed and true, aimed by angel hands, failed to penetrate"—*Christ's Object Lessons*, p. 160. He could never see himself—his own need—until he saw his God!

The Seventh-day Adventist Church as a whole—and every individual member in particular—is clearly profiled in Scripture. We have already been diagnosed by the One who knows all and always tells the truth. "I know your deeds, that you are neither cold nor hot. I wish you were one or the other! . . . You say, 'I am rich; I have acquired wealth and do not need a thing.' But you do not realize that you are wretched, pitiful, poor, blind and naked" (Revelation 3:15, 17). We may castigate the Pharisee for his stubborn refusal to see his true condition—he is safely frozen in a distant-past time frame—but that will not make our case any better.

Scripture contains some powerful case histories. We must not only read the Bible—we must allow the Bible to read us. Look at Isaiah. Young, talented, of noble birth, he reported: "I saw the Lord seated on a throne, high and exalted, and the train of his robe filled the temple." Isaiah's immediate response? "Woe to me! I am ruined! For I am a man of unclean lips, and I live among a people of unclean lips, and my eyes have seen the King, the Lord Almighty" (Isaiah 6:1, 5).

This is ultimate reality—to see the King. But seeing the King made Isaiah feel wretched. The experience was chastening. There could be no self-deception in the glaring light of God's revealing presence. Isaiah was in a bad way. He saw himself as inadequate and sinful. Throwing his undeserving soul on the mercy of this holy God, he received grace, pardon, and forgiveness. Isaiah's story is our story—all humanity's story.

After the shock of seeing ourselves as we are—and as God sees us—healing, restoration, and the renewed communication can begin. "Come, let us return unto the Lord. He has torn us to pieces but he will heal us; he has injured us but he will bind up our wounds. After two days he will revive us, that we may live in his presence" (Hosea 6:1, 2).

God-shaped Emptiness

One reality of the human condition is universal. Augustine and other religious writers speak about a God-shaped emptiness at the center of every human being—a space only God can fill. After all, we are more than bone and muscle and brain cells. We are created in the image of God. Things, possessions, will never satisfy us. Jesus told us that "Man does not live on bread alone" (Matthew 4:4). Our humanity demands more than food and raiment to sustain and fulfill us—to make us complete. This fulfillment comes instead by "every word that comes from the mouth of God" (Matthew 4:4). The biblical account indicates that we were created for communion with our Creator.

We are inadequate to meet the demands of life on our own. The strongest among us is at times terrified at the prospect of coping with life's stresses and uncertainties. Future shock—that rapid acceleration in the pace of change that makes it seem the future has arrived prematurely—leaves us feeling inadequate, overwhelmed, and threatened. Our inability to control our lives leaves us feeling frustrated. "Tis all in pieces," said John Donne, "all coherence gone." The poet Yeats remarked: "Things fall apart, the center cannot hold." As the lyrics of the popular song put it, "People need the Lord." We sense the need of a Power out of and beyond ourselves to help us cope.

Peter Berger, the sociologist, coined an expression to describe this reality. He called it "subterranean rumblings of supernaturalism." Berger reports that "in a study of American students, 80 per cent of the respondents expressed a 'need for religious faith,' while only 48 percent admitted to a belief in God in traditional Judaeo-Christian terms." A similar study in western Germany was more striking: "69 percent said that they believed in God—but 86 per cent admitted to praying!"—Peter Berger, *A Rumor of Angels*, Doubleday, p. 30.

We do not believe in what the theologians call "natural religion" (that every individual has deep within a religious impulse that can be developed though human effort). What we do believe is that the need to reach out to a higher Power is universal. Sociologists who study religion are amazed to find it in every culture, ancient and modern. It cuts across all lines. A San Francisco newspaper ran a story about Chairman Kruschev's visit to the United States in the early 70s. When the bus he was riding in suddenly swerved toward a precipice, the leader of what was then the greatest atheistic country in the world cried out, "Lord, have mercy!" In moments of extremity, even atheists think of prayer.

All that we have said above squares with the biblical account that God created the human race "so that men would seek him and perhaps find him, though he is not far from each one of us." There is something in us, a divine programming, that prompts us to want to be in contact with the Almighty. "For in him we live and move and have our being." We are talking about a basic need—a fundamental reality. Paul was speaking to a pagan audience when he said, "We are his offspring" (Acts 17:27, 28).

Find out about God

To find out about prayer is to find out about God. The God of the Bible is a personal being. Powerful beyond description (omnipotent), all wise and all knowing (omniscient), and present everywhere at the same time (omnipresent), He nevertheless has an interest in and concern for every human being on the earth. He takes delight in communicating with us. He even pursues us. He is kind, compassionate, gracious, merciful, longsuffering, has unlimited patience, and is generous. "God is love" (1 John

4:8). He has gone to great lengths to open up the channel of communication between earth and heaven.

There is a science of prayer. When we use the word *science* in this sense, we mean that there is some rhyme or reason or order. There are laws that govern its operation. Aided by the Holy Spirit, it is possible to know something about even the deep things, the mysteries, of God. As the Bible uses the word, *mystery* means some deep spiritual truth that the human mind, unaided by the Spirit, cannot possibly comprehend. The oft-quoted text, "No eye has seen, no ear has heard, no mind has conceived what God has prepared for those who love him" (1 Corinthians 2:9) does not apply exclusively to the New Earth experience. Its primary emphasis is on the experience of knowing God in the here and now.

> "The Spirit searches all things, even the deep things of God . . . no one knows the thoughts of God except the Spirit of God. We have not received the spirit of the world but the Spirit who is from God that we may understand what God has freely given us" (1 Corinthians 2:10-12).

The great throne-room vision of Revelation 4 and 5 dramatically portrays the complexity and sophistication of heaven's intergalactic communication system. The prophet is in the Spirit and sees heaven opened, veils and curtains drawn. There is "a throne in heaven with someone sitting on it" (Revelation 4:2). He sees the rainbow of promise—the assurance of God's faithfulness—and the twenty-four elders, "purchased men for God." The angelic host praise God for His great creation and His marvelous redemption. The Lamb approaches the throne and takes the book of destiny from the Occupant. Our hearts throb with John's as he takes in the scene. Father, Son, and Holy Spirit are joined in the work of creation and redemption.

What takes place now expands the horizons of our

understanding; heaven is all about communication—about God's receiving and considering our prayers, our petitions, even our complaints. The Old Testament typology has the smoke ascending from the altar of incense and wafting into the Most Holy Place. But in the original sanctuary above, the angels are seen assisting: "Each one had a harp and they were holding golden bowls full of incense, which are the prayers of the saints" (Revelation 5:8). In Revelation, chapter 8, we have the same scene:

> "Another angel, who had a golden censer, came and stood at the altar. He was given much incense to offer, with the prayers of all the saints, on the golden altar before the throne" (Revelation 8:3).

These are mysterious, highly symbolic representations of great realities. The human mind cannot grasp the full implications of it all, but we begin to see, if ever so dimly, that central to the plan of redemption is the ministry of presenting the prayers of God's earthly family members to the Father. The process is integral to the whole work of salvation. And this sacred activity goes on until probation closes, when the angel throws down the golden censer (verse 5).

Royal invitation

What boggles the mind about prayer is that this all-powerful God calls me to engage in ongoing conversation with Him, and He has established a fail-safe system to personally assure me of instant and constant communication with Him. "In him [Christ] and through faith in him we may approach God with freedom and confidence" (Ephesians 3:12).

I am not just an uninvolved bystander. I am the object of divine solicitude—of God's exclusive focus. It is my prayers that are ascending. I have a personal stake in all this.

In ancient times the common people entered the presence of the king at the peril of their lives, and it was unthinkable to go into the throne room unbidden. What a relief it was when the king reached forth his scepter so they could touch it—a gesture of acceptance. If we can believe it, prayer takes us into the throne room of the monarch of the universe. And the scepter is always stretched forth! What is more, He has invited us, even urged us, to come. "Come all of you who are thirsty, come to the waters . . ." (Isaiah 55:1). "If anyone is thirsty, let him come to me and drink" (John 7:37). "The Spirit and the bride say 'Come'" (Revelation 22:17).

"If radio's slim fingers can pluck a melody from night—
And toss it over a continent or sea;
If the petalled white notes of violins are blown
Across the mountains or the city's din;
If songs, like crimson roses, are called from thin blue air—
Why should mortals wonder if God hears prayer?"
—Ethel Romig Fuller

Find out about the Son

But we have a problem. This audience chamber is off limits to sinful human beings, and we have already been diagnosed as terribly unworthy. We cannot come into His presence without a mediator—someone who can touch both divinity and humanity. One has been found! A Mediator has been provided! The great God who calls us to prayer has seen to this. In our quest to find out about prayer, we must focus on the real Christ—the Christ of the Bible—not some illusory phantom of our imagination. We find this accurate picture of Jesus only in Scripture, not in icons or religious art or mood music—or even in beautiful scenes of nature. The real Jesus is not portrayed in "Jesus Christ, Superstar." We cannot fully depend even on the finest and most gifted human authors. They are in some ways helpful, but they are not the ultimate in portraying Jesus. We must have the authentic picture—"The light of the knowledge of the glory of God in the face of Jesus" (2 Corinthians 4:6). For this portrait, we go to the Bible.

"The Son is the radiance of God's glory and the exact representation of his being" (Hebrews 1:3). When we see the Son, we have already seen the Father. (See John 14:9.)

S.D. Gordon, a pastor in Boston at the turn of the century, was on target when he said, "Jesus is God's thought made audible, God's speech made intelligible, and God's form made visible. Jesus is God spelling Himself out to man in language that man can understand." To focus is to adjust the lens so that the object of our attention comes into clearer view.

The Word helps us focus properly. Indeed, as James Houston says, "The most important aid to prayer is to make our own exploration in the Bible."—*The Transforming Friendship*, p. 36. Ellen White calls the application of the Word the eyesalve that sharpens our vision. Meditating on the Word is a kind of communion or communication. We hear a voice!

Jesus is truly God and truly man. He is representative man. As a true priest—the only functioning true priest in all the world, in fact—He goes to the Father on our behalf. In His humanity, He touches and is touched by us; in His divinity, He is in perfect relationship with God. "In the beginning was the Word, and the Word was with God, and the Word was God" (John 1:1). The original language behind this verse suggests the idea that He was always "turned toward God."

Because the communication system between earth and heaven was broken by Adam's sin, God gave Him to the human family to become "bone of our bone and flesh of our flesh," thus reestablishing the broken connection. It is as one of us that He approaches the throne of Deity. "For there is one mediator between God and men, the man Christ Jesus" (1 Timothy 2:5). He has always been the

God between. The throne-room vision continues to be instructive. "Then I saw a Lamb, looking as if it had been slain, standing in the center of the throne, encircled by the four living creatures and the twenty-four elders" (Revelation 5:5).

At what great cost has God reestablished the broken connection! A slain Lamb, His own Son, was required to again establish the contact. "Though earth was struck off from the continent of heaven and alienated from its communion, Jesus has connected it again with the sphere of glory"—*Sons and Daughters of God*, p. 244. His testimony to His disciples was that "no one comes to the Father except through me" (John 14:6). There can be no effective prayer without Him.

Effective prayer has everything to do with understanding who Jesus is and what His role and function is in the plan of salvation. He is our great High Priest. "He always lives to intercede for them [us]" (Hebrews 7:25). He is Jacob's ladder. "I tell you the truth, you shall see heaven open, and the angels of God ascending and descending upon the Son of Man" (John 1:51). He offers our prayers to the Father mingled with His merits and moist with His shed blood.

The will to prepare

A news reporter once said to a great long-distance runner after he had just won a grueling marathon race, "You must have a great will to win. "Yes, I do," he replied. "but the will to win is easy—it is the will to prepare that is difficult!"

I am optimistic. A dynamic prayer life is within our reach. The question is, are we willing to discipline ourselves, to put ourselves to the test, in order to achieve it? Discipline is the basic tool we need. Without it, there can be no solution to our spiritual dilemma.

"It will require a determined heart and more than a little courage," observes A.W. Tozer, "to wrench ourselves loose from the grip of our own times and return to biblical ways" (A.W. Tozer, *The Pursuit of God*, p. 70).

> "So I say to you: Ask and it will be given you; seek and you will find; knock and the door will be opened unto you. For everyone who asks receives; he who seeks finds; and to him who knocks, the door will be opened" (Luke 11:9, 10).

Let's make the investment.

2

Working Through the Myths

"Now this is eternal life: that they may know you the true God and Jesus Christ whom you have sent" (John 17:3).

Our prayer life must be based on truth, not misconceptions, illusions, and myths. We need a solid foundation. We need to be aware of the realities. And we need to work our way through a great many myths and misconceptions about prayer. These myths are both obvious and subtle, stubborn, persistent, and widespread. They skew our prayer life.

"It is the darkness of misapprehension of the character of God that is enshrouding the world. Men are losing their knowledge of His character. It has been misunderstood and misinterpreted"
—*Christ's Object Lessons,* p. 424.

Let's not think we are immune from or entirely free from the influence of these myths. Such fictions operate in religious circles too. Until we clear away this underbrush, our own prayer lives will be shallow and unfulfilling.

Most of these myths stem from a false concept of God. In our society, God is caricatured, cartooned, and stereotyped. He is painted either as a pathetic, rather nice old man who nobody takes seriously or as a mean tyrant who tortures children and makes innocent people suffer. This may be an extreme way of putting it, but it serves to highlight the reality. The pity is that religous people aid and abet these distortions by monstrous doctrines such as that of an eternally burning hell. One extreme is as bad as the other.

Our concept of God means everything to our prayer life. These myths prove to be mists that can be cleared away just as the low-lying clouds are dissipated by the rising sun. One thing is certain: God is no cosmic bully. It is "those who are deceived by Satan" who "look upon God as hard and exacting" and who "regard Him as watching to denounce and condemn. . . . unwilling to receive the sinner so long as there is legal excuse for not helping him"—*Christ's Object Lessons*, p. 207.

God is a parent

Jesus' favorite theme was the paternal nature of the character of God. It is as if He wanted to say to the whole world, "Let me tell you about my Father." This picture of God is central to the sermon on the mount and a number of the parables. It is a familiar theme also in the Old Testament. The God of Israel is a loving parent, full of compassion toward His erring children, "for He knows how we are formed, he remembers that we are dust" (Psalm 103:13). The prophets report His great concern for us: "Can a mother forget the baby at her breast and have no compassion on the child she has borne? Though she may forget, I will not forget you" (Isaiah 49:15).

"How can I give you up? . . . My compassion is aroused, I will not carry out my fierce anger . . . I will not come in wrath" (Hosea 11:8).

Jesus authorizes us to use the name that the children in a family use to address their earthly fathers. In His day, that was *abba*. It could be "dad" in our culture, or "papa" in other parts of the world. It would be totally out of place for anyone but a family member to use such an intimate form of address. While God was looked on as a Father in Old Testament times, no prophet ever thought of speaking to the Almighty in this manner. It remained for the Son to bring this astounding revelation. Some of the finest biblical scholars maintain that this is the most revolutionary concept ever introduced into human thought.

Paul exclaims, "For you did not receive a spirit that makes you a slave again to fear, but you received the Spirit of sonship. And by him we cry, Abba, Father" (Romans 8:15).

Although He is all kindness and love, the God we serve has an unyielding hatred for sin. His holiness is awesome. There is no way that He could ever compromise with sin. He alone understands how deadly and toxic sin is. Sugarcoating sin makes it all the more dangerous. The tendency in some religious circles is to cheapen grace to the point where the law of God is made of no effect. This is the problem with modern theology. Thus you have, to paraphrase one of yesterday's religious writers, a God without wrath who brings men without sin into a kingdom without judgment through the ministry of a Christ without a cross. This flabby, watered-down theology leads to a puny, powerless prayer life.

A contemporary theologian puts it aptly:

> "Of course, Jesus did not want to proclaim anything like an ambiguous private God or an indeterminate psuedo-modern belief in God . . . that unassuming God of bourgeois mediocrity

> who corresponds to our very selective, favorite moral ideas, having no disturbing features and making no inconvenient demands; a God who simply takes people where they are and allows them to stay in their selfish ways; who is more than satisfied when we acknowledge his existence and who will never hurt anyone, since he understands and therefore pardons everything. In brief, this is a God who harms no one, but also thus makes possible a kind of 'religion' which disturbs nothing and imposes no obligation"—Hans Kung, *On Being a Christian*, pp. 295, 296.

Devout Christians of a bygone era used imposing words to speak about the greatness of God and His mighty power. You still see some of these words in the old hymns—high-sounding words like *indescribable, inexpressible, nameless, transcendent, unspeakable, unutterable, ineffable.* The "Wholly Other" is a term more in vogue these days.

All these terms attempt to describe what is not easily comprehended. We need to be tongue-tied in the presence of supreme mystery. The bane of modern thinking is its tendency to reduce God to human dimensions. In an age of scientific wonders, we want to master the data and come out with a precise formula. But God defies all human attempts to measure Him.

Job's question is still fitting: "Can you fathom the mysteries of God? Can you probe the limits of the Almighty?" (Job 11:7). The last message of mercy that goes to Planet Earth is about the majesty and greatness of God. "Fear God and give him glory, because the hour of his judgment has come. Worship him who made the heavens, the earth, the sea, and the springs of water" (Revelation 14:7). This is timely and relevant to our discussion. J. B. Phillips, the Bible translator, captured our tendency to diminish God in the title of one of his books—*Your God Is Too Small.*

A couple of decades ago, a delightful little story made the rounds among the preachers. As I remember, it was about a little girl who was drawing a picture. "What are you drawing?" someone asked her. "A picture of God" was her answer. "But nobody knows what God looks like" said her questioner. To which she replied, "They will when I get through!"

Our God is too small if we think we can describe Him. The God of Abraham, Isaac, and Jacob is beyond the range of human language. The happy paradox is that in spite of our inability to adequately describe Him, we can nevertheless know Him by experience.

His holiness

We must talk more about the holiness of God and the holiness He would have us attain if the quality of our prayer life is to be radically improved. Holiness is agreement with God, wholeness for God. Biblical holiness is not ecstasy, or as they say, warm fuzzies. Nor is it that kind of perfection that parades its own goodness and applauds its attainments. It is total commitment to God—solidarity with Him, His plans and purposes. It is looking to Him at all times for guidance and support in every situation.

This is what the Old Testament saints called walking with God. It is maintaining a sense of awe and wonder at His absolute purity and at the same time clinging to the hope that He is a God of mercy and compassion. "Yet he does not leave the guilty unpunished" (Exodus 34:7). His wrath is the temperature of His love.

Strange outcomes

Without this solid, biblically based concept of God, prayer can take on some strange unchristian aspects that lead to curious outcomes. It could even become a kind of magic—a way of manipulating God and attempting to get Him to do what we want Him to do. "And when you pray, do not keep on babbling like the pagans, for they think that they will be heard because of their many words" (Matthew 6:7). More words, more vigorous turning of the prayer wheel, more beating of the breast, and maybe the Almighty will be impressed and moved to hear and answer. He must be appeased. We must bring Him some gifts or He will be angry. Could it be that Christians are affected to some degree by these misapprehensions?

> "Magic can appear more subtly in the prayers of people who would be horrified to think that they were involved in magic. It is alarmingly easy for prayer to become a kind of magical device which we use to get our own way" (Houston, p. 30).

Out of this major myth arises a host of other false concepts. One of these is that prayer is a wish list or a shopping list. Another makes prayer primarily crisis intervention, to be used only in times of extremity. (When everything else fails, try prayer.) Still another is what someone has called the God-in-a-box belief. This was the Israelites' problem. They thought that God was actually contained in the ark and looked on the sacred chest with superstitious awe.

Of course, God is not a genie in a bottle who responds to some magic word or touch. He "does not live in temples built by hands" (Acts 17:24). He is not the God of shrines. "God is spirit, and his worshippers must worship in spirit and in truth" (John 4:25). Further, we need to be wary of overdependence on "aids to worship" either visual or oral. "You shall not make for yourself an idol in the form of anything in heaven above or in the waters below" (Exodus 20:4). "The attempt to represent the Eternal One by a material object would lower man's conception of God"—*Patriarchs and Prophets,* p. 306. Israel's God is known only by revelation—through His Word. We are a Word-centered community.

When we clear away the stubborn underbrush, we are well on the way to the realization that prayer is as normal to the Christian life as is breathing. It is not an added ingredient—something tacked on at the end of a day of busy activities. And while it may be as normal as breathing, it is absolutely as necessary to spiritual life as breath is to the body.

To the committed believer, prayer is a deepening friendship, an extended conversation with our Maker and our King. It is free and open communication between friends walking together in complete agreement. What a fellowship! "He has showed you, O man what is good. And what does the Lord require of you? To act justly and to love mercy and to walk humbly with your God" (Micah 6:8).

C.S. Lewis became a Christian after establishing a reputation as a world-class scholar at Oxford. His friends and colleagues thought he had gone "daft." As a new convert, he had a terrible struggle in developing an effective prayer life. How can one talk to someone unseen and unheard? Especially was this struggle difficult for a man of letters. It taxes one's credibility, his friends said. But Lewis was determined to find out about prayer and was rewarded, as are all who "diligently seek Him." Out of this experience there came a poem entitled simply "Prayer":

Master, they say that when I seem
To be in speech with you,
Since you make no replies, it's all a dream
—One talker aping two.

They are half right but not as they
Imagine; rather, I
Seek in myself the things I meant to say,
And lo the wells are dry.

Then seeing me empty, you forsake
The listener's role, and through

My dead lips breathe and into utterance wake
The thoughts I never knew.

We need to be reparented. And then we need an orientation into our new family, its customs and ways. We need to become better acquainted with the members of the family—our family tree, our roots. But most of all, we need to know our Father, His Son our elder brother, and the Holy Spirit—our special Counselor and traveling companion. Prayer is the learning environment that He has provided for our training and instruction.

3

Overcoming the Obstacles

"Then the man said, your name will no longer be Jacob, but Israel, because you have struggled with God and with men and you have overcome" (Genesis 32:28).

Prayer in the hectic, pressurized 90s is no luxury—it is an absolute necessity. Yet this life of prayer is difficult at best. Keeping up our prayer life is like going through an obstacle course. Those who pray are going against prevailing culture; they are bucking the tide. Everything about modern life is hostile to spirituality. This is not a prayer-friendly culture.

It's been said that any old dead fish can float downstream, but it takes a live one to swim against the stream. If we are going to buck the tide, it will take a made-up mind. "This calls for patient endurance on part of the saints" (Revelation 14:12). We will have to make a conscious decision that we are going to break through the impasse. It won't be easy, but we have some mighty helpers on our side.

The little woman and the tough judge

"Then Jesus told his disciples a story to show them that they should always pray and never give up" (Luke 18:1). The story He told is about a tough judge. This judge doesn't care about anybody. He is heartless. In his court, it's the law and no breaks for anyone. That's just the way it is. He was certainly no bleeding-heart liberal!

One day a little old grandmother comes before him with a complaint. She has been wronged. So what's new, the judge thinks. My docket is filled with nuisance suits. These lawyers! Nothing about her impresses him. She is a nobody. He will get through this one really fast.

But he doesn't know this little old lady. She hangs in there, because she knows her cause is right. Nothing the judge says can shake her. It is getting to be embarrassing. His fellow judges are beginning to snicker. The wiseacres around the courtroom are making jokes. Mr. Toughie can't take it any longer. Alright, Madam, he finally says in desperation, what is it you want? OK—you have it! Now, please, just get out of my court!

The disciples got the point, and we do to. Jesus is talking about perseverance. The woman was ready to bed down at city hall for as long as it took to get justice. If it's worth it, it's worth hanging in there for it. The emphasis is not on the judge but on the petitioner. The emphasis is on us—are we willing to overcome the obstacles? Is it worth it? You had better believe it! "Let us throw off everything that hinders and the sin that so easily entangles, and let us run with perseverance the race marked out for us" (Hebrews 12:1).

There are all kinds of obstacles to surmount, all manner of distractions and deterrents to spiritual growth. Let's face it, most of us are tired and stressed out.

Some of the most important messages Jesus gave come to us through His second-coming parables. Theologians call them the parousia parables. They speak to our particular situation, our peculiar problems, as if they had been written this morning. They tell us what to watch for. You find these parables in Matthew 24, Mark 13, and Luke 21.

What makes them so much to the point is that they are addressed to our times, our special circumstances. This is an uncharted time—an unmeasured time. All the great time prophecies have met their fulfillment. There are no more prophetic dates looming ahead. Ellen White clearly states: "There will never again be a message for the people that will be based on time"—*Selected Messages,* book 1, p. 188. Of course, there are signs of Christ's coming, but no one knows the day or the hour.

And while it is true that "The angels of God in their messages to men represent time as very short" (*Selected Messages*, book 1, p. 67), we have no way of calculating how many years or months or weeks remain. Jesus knew this would be a difficult time, so He gave us some special instructions, warnings and counsel.

On guard!

On guard, be alert (Mark 13:33), Jesus says to us. "Be careful, or your hearts will be weighed down with dissipation, drunkenness and the anxieties of life, and that day will come on you unexpectedly like a trap" (Luke 21:34). Jesus is trying to tell us that our number one problem will be spiritual fatigue.

Rabbi Marc Tannenbaum brought this message back from Israel after one of his visits there. "The big problem is fatigue," he said, "brought on by the long struggle." Throughout the second-coming parables, Jesus beams His message to people who are in danger of falling asleep. "The bridegroom was a long time in coming, and they all became drowsy and fell asleep" (Matthew 25:5).

The biggest obstacle to prayer is spiritual fatigue—

sleep. Which leads us to conclude that the major hurdle in this obstacle course is ourselves. We have met the enemy, and "they is us!" We will make no spiritual progress if we simply wring our hands and complain about how hard it is to keep up our prayer life. We will have to begin with ourselves.

We are too busy and distracted. James Houston talks about "the narcotic of busyness" and the "poverty of affluence." Most of us, he says, are caught up in "this rat race we call life." We are caught on a treadmill. In love with things—possessions—and seduced by the sensate, we can scarcely stay awake for an hour of prayer and Bible study on a given evening.

Let's face it, we are in many ways "out of it" when it comes to spiritual things. And let's not get into denial, because denial will get us nowhere. The facts remain the same. The advice Christ gives the Laodiceans (another way of saying us—this is *our* profile) is to "be earnest and repent" (Revelation 3:19).

Repentance is a good, sturdy biblical word. It is the turning point at which we begin to think differently about spiritual things. Repentance is a defining moment, when we "come to ourselves." Repentance involves radical change—total reorientation of the life, a change of direction 180 degrees. Repentance is one of those times when we can say "From this day onward!" Repentance is a new beginning. It's the only way to make a fresh start—a clean break with the past.

What to do? How to begin? Block out some quality time. I did not say some free time, because the tendency is to say, I don't have any. Clear the decks. Turn off the phone. "Go into your room," Jesus says, "close the door and pray to your Father, who is unseen" (Matthew 6:6). We cannot improve on the divine counsel. Rule or step number one—carve out a block of time and hold it inviolate. Make a solemn commitment.

Navy people have a saying, "You can't turn a battleship

on a dime." We can't get out of this web, this terrible fix we are in, in an instant. But we have to make a start. Repent! Take hold of the steering wheel. Grab the rudder and turn it hard!

The struggle goes on

Now we are ready to tackle the obstacles. And what are they? Let's personalize them:

"I'm so tired."
"I get terribly sleepy."
"But my mind wanders, and I can't focus."
"I hate to admit it, but it does get boring."
"How do I avoid all those distractions?"

We need to understand what's going on—where good intentions and earthly realities interface. This is a never-ending struggle. Why is it that we *will* to do but come up short on performance? Paul recognized this and admitted that "in my inner members I delight in God's law; but I see another law at work in the members of my body" (Romans 7:23). Again, here is the big obstacle. All the others stem from it. It is spirit versus flesh or body. We remember Jesus' words to His disciples: "The spirit is willing, but the body is weak" (Matthew 26:41).

It is not just that we are in a physical body—we *are* a physical body. We are bony structure, and skin, and glands, and hormones, and systems (cardiovascular and nervous), brain cells, and chemicals. The point is, we are physical. The only way heaven can communicate with us is through the sensory parts of this body and its capital, the brain.

But for all its glory and wonder—and we *are* fearfully and wonderfully made (see Psalm 139)—the body is weak, deranged by sin, and burdened with the legacy of 6,000 years of sinful history. People who pray effectively know this in a profound way. Even Elijah, who was translated, "was a man just like us" (James 5:17). The prophets and holy men and women were not exempt.

No two alike

Each of us is an individual. No two of us are exactly alike. The behavioral scientists tell us that there are certain general personality types and temperaments. We have all heard about the Type A and Type B people—the highly motivated achievers and the laid-back, easygoing kind. Some of us are morning creatures, and some of us are nocturnal. We need to build our prayer lives with this in mind, taking advantage of "peak times." We also need to know that some of us are more emotional than others, while some are more rational. This knowledge can be helpful as we evaluate our prayer life.

> "Temperament is the vitality we inherit in our central nervous system, our hormonal balance, and all the other ways in which our body influences our moods, thoughts and feelings" (Houston, p. 129).

There are four generally recognized temperaments: the *sanguine*, the *phlegmatic*, the *choleric*, and the *melancholy*. One Christian psychologist told me there are at least twelve. I am not sufficiently informed to comment specifically. This is a book on prayer, not psychology. But suffice it to say that it helps to know how we work, what makes us tick, the dynamics and chemistry of these complex beings that we are. Most important is to recognize that we have to work with what we have, what we are.

Each of these temperaments probably responds to God and spiritual things in a distinctive manner. James Houston believes that sanguine persons become restless after more than ten minutes in prayer because they are the active type. Conversely, phlegmatic people develop a structured prayer life more readily, because they are generally more stable and conservative. Cholerics are thought to be logical and rational and not very emotional, so that relationships are not developed easily. Melancholies are creative and imaginative, reflective and thoughtful, and tend to be more spontaneous in their prayers—though not as systematic.

The good news is that we are not locked into the past. No matter what our personality or temperament, change is possible. Prayer is a transforming fellowship! Whatever the case, we cannot make excuses and blame any lack of progress in our prayer lives on temperament or personality.

God must indeed revel in variety. Like the snowflake, there are no two identical individuals. There is no psychological model that fits even one person perfectly. We develop in an endless number of ways. We respond differently to similar sets of circumstances and experiences. We are distinct and singular. No one is qualified to prescribe another's prayer life.

Beware of guru types who tell others in great detail how to go about their personal spiritual formation. We are responsible beings, accountable to God alone for the development of our life in the Spirit. We find what is best for us and follow on to know the Lord "in our own way." C.S. Lewis was right when he said, "There are no ordinary people. You have never talked to a mere mortal" (quoted in James Houston, *The Transforming Fellowship*, p. 15). Every person is a unique creation of God.

We are not always at our peak times. The mind does wander. These distractions do come. But not to worry. The main thing is to be open to God and spiritual things. The times I don't feel like praying are the times I need to pray in spite of my feelings.

What we are trying to do is establish patterns and good prayer habits. David vowed to pray morning, noon, and night. There may be no great feeling of ecstasy, but we are building a solid foundation of practice that will stand us in good stead. "I always stay prayed up," the great evangelist D.L. Moody used to say. It is good, in times of sudden emergency, to know where to turn and to know that place so well that we turn to it as naturally as the "flower to the sun."

Name change

The man Jacob was a supplanter, a "heel grabber," Scripture says. They could have nicknamed him Slick Jake. (All of the personality types can be seen in the Bible.) But there came a time when Jacob faced up to the truth about himself. He refused to make any excuses for his past conduct. His repentance was thorough and deep. Jesus made a night appointment with him at Jabbock. It was a mysterious confrontation that can be fully understood only by experience.

> "Not a word was spoken, but Jacob put forth all his strength, and did not relax his efforts for a moment. . . . The struggle continued until near the break of day, when the stranger placed his finger upon Jacob's thigh, and he was crippled instantly. . . . disabled and suffering the keenest pain, he would not loosen his hold. . . . his faith more earnest and persevering, until the very last"—*Patriarchs and Prophets*, p. 197.

In his extremity, the patriarch cried out, "I will not let you go until you bless me" (Genesis 32:26). And he was blessed, and his name was changed, because he overcame. And the story is recorded for those of us who also face obstacles today. (See Romans 15:4.)

Just before us is the great time of trouble. Already, the earth is coming apart at the seams. Everywhere we see the cumulative effects of sin's reign. In the words of the old spiritual, "If we ever needed the Lord before, we sure do need Him now." There is no magic formula, no easy way, to spiritual power. The "world" will always be unfriendly; it is not yet "a friend of grace to help us on to God."

Prayer develops mental toughness—like a workout at

the gym. Pious Jews and Christians of yesteryear spoke of prayer as being hard labor. Prayer prepares us for the stern realities of life. Prayer strengthens the moral fiber. These are the very qualities we all need for living in these days.

Remember the little old woman (she is us), and remember the tough judge (he does not represent God). He gave in only because the woman wore him out. Our heavenly Father never tires of our coming. "If you, then, though you are evil, know how to give good gifts to your children, how much more will your Father in heaven give good gifts to those who ask him" (Matthew 7:11).

Take heart. We shall overcome. There is a new name for each of us that reflects our peculiar experience. "To him who overcomes, I will also give him a white stone with a new name written on it, known only to him who receives it" (Revelation 2:12).

4

The Prayer Life of Jesus

"One day Jesus was praying in a certain place. When he finished, one of his disciples said to him, 'Lord teach us to pray, just as John taught his disciples'" (Luke 11:1).

"The intercession of Christ is a golden chain fastened to the throne of God. He has turned the merit of His sacrifice into prayer. Jesus prays and by prayer succeeds."—*S.D.A. Bible Commentary*, vol. 7, p. 914.

Jesus' prayer life was perfect, which is to say that He was always in sync with His Father. No one else who ever lived achieved this complete rapport with God. He is the role model for all times and seasons. No human being can ever come close to the great Exemplar. But this does not mean we are to aim any lower than the example He set. We must strive to reach the mark. I haven't made it yet, Paul said, but "I press on toward the goal . . . " (Philippians 3:14).

Jesus left us an example in blocking out periods of "quality time." "Very early in the morning, while it was still dark, Jesus got up, left the house and went off to a solitary place where he prayed" (Mark 1:35). Jesus was what He taught. He was truth in flesh. He lived the words He spoke. With Him there was never the slightest inconsistency between word and deed. In fact, with Jesus, word and deed were—and are—the same. "He spoke and it was done." He alone could say, "truly, truly I say to you," because He is truth. He is the Amen of God.

Time and place

Just as He told us to do, He cleared away a space in time and a place—a "closet." Our Savior had no home of His own, so He claimed the woods, the field, the mountain. He overcame the obstacles, established His position, and took charge of circumstances. There is no better example. Think of His childhood home circumstances. A simple peasant's cottage, dirt floor, annoying siblings, work from dawn till dusk, home chores—we could go on and on. Not the most conducive atmosphere to spiritual growth, you will admit. Yet in spite of it all, "Jesus grew in wisdom and stature, and in favor with God and men" (Luke 2:52).

His life was one, unbroken, uninterrupted prayer. It was perpetual communion. His conversation with His Father never ceased. There were no down times in Jesus' system. It was always ready, up, and running. He had very little seclusion. He never had the luxury of a private room. The crowds, sometimes friendly, sometimes hostile, were always there. Getting time for meals was not easy.

Scanning the gospel of Mark, where the emphasis is on action and doing, gives us a sense of what a day in the life of Jesus was like. In a single chapter (the 6th), we see intense activity—healing, teaching, preaching, crowds, hecklers in the crowd, interruptions. As we read, we begin to see a pattern—certain breaks in the busy agenda.

> "Then because so many people were coming and going that they did not have chance to eat, he said to them, 'Come with me by yourselves to a quiet place and get some rest'" (Mark 6:31).

"After leaving them, he went up on a mountainside to pray" (Mark 6:46). We do need to be alone, but we must carve out some time. "Steal away," the spiritual says, "steal away to Jesus."

We want to pray like that

Any wonder that the disciples asked Him to teach them how to pray? His prayer life was so rewarding, so real. He obviously enjoyed talking to His Father. Sometimes He was so absorbed in deep communication with the Father that He was unaware of anything around Him. "Lord, teach us to pray" (Luke 11:2) one of them asked Him. They had the matchless Man of prayer with them. They saw Him in conversation with His Father. They saw Him draw on inexhaustible resources.

Jesus of Nazareth is the embodiment of all that the prophets and apostles had to say about prayer itself and about the prayer experience of those noble men and women of the Bible who prayed so effectively. Abraham, Moses, and Samuel offered mighty prayers of intercession. David urged God to arise and defend Himself against His enemies, because he was zealous for His glory. Elijah prayed that Yahweh would reveal Himself in defense of truth. Jeremiah's ardent prayers were for wandering, backslidden Israel to hear the Word of the Lord.

It pleased God to disclose, in the experience of the Old Testament worthies, some of the qualities that would make up the rich prayer life of Jesus. Our Savior stands at the top of the roster, gathering up in His person all that is good in the "law and the prophets."

What is most impressive to me is that Jesus gave me a personal example for my prayer life that fits my special needs. When we see Him, we see what God intended for us to be. This is why I am not intimidated by Jesus' perfect performance, as I would be by the exhibition of a great superstar on the same playing field with me. I am overwhelmed by this perfect Man, but I am not discouraged or cast down because of His perfection. Not as I would be if I were surrounded with genius and super talent and truly gifted people—they seem so far above the ordinary, above my level of life.

But somehow, Jesus in all His absolute perfection seems to be saying to me, This is what I want you to do. This is how I want you to live. Somehow, I begin to sense that what He did and who He was when He was here on earth relates to me and what I can be. He did come down to my level and accept my lot. He achieved as a human being. He did not come as a world-class spiritual athlete to "show off." He came to assure me that weak and erring mortals such as myself could come to know God in a saving way. He always leaves me with hope. "Be of good cheer," He says. "I have overcome." With men this is impossible, but with God, all things are possible. The perfect Jesus is not a threat—He is a promise! I hope you feel that way too.

Model prayer

The great lesson to be gained from Jesus' prayer life is His complete surrender, submission, and obedience to His Father's will. The conclusive manifestation of this is seen in His prayer in the garden of Gethsemane. Always, it was His Father's will. "Father, if it is not possible for this cup to be taken away except I drink it, may your will be done" (Matthew 26:42).

The Master taught a great many things about prayer.

He gave us a model prayer, which we should analyze and explore. Some of our Bible teachers remind us that this is not in the strictest sense the Lord's prayer—it is the disciples' prayer.

In the briefest space, He gives us a comprehensive course in the theology of prayer. He enunciates eight principles—constituent elements that should be included in our prayers: Adoration, Thanksgiving, Affirmation, Forgiveness, Renewal, Personal needs, Others' needs, and How to bring our prayers to a close.

If this is the prayer we are to go by, then we should examine ourselves in its light. How do we measure up? How do our prayers stand up against the model prayer? The only acceptable prayer is that prayer which is offered in the spirit and manner of the prayer Jesus taught us to pray.

Many years ago someone shared a selection with me entitled "Can you say the Lord's prayer?"

Can You Say the Lord's Prayer?

I cannot say "OUR" if I live in a watertight spiritual compartment.

I cannot say "FATHER" if I do not demonstrate the relationship in daily life.

I cannot say "THY KINGDOM COME" if I am not doing what I can to hasten its coming.

I cannot say "THY WILL BE DONE" if I am questioning, resentful or disobedient to His will for me.

I cannot say "ON EARTH AS IT IS IN HEAVEN" if I am not prepared to devote my life to His service.

I cannot say "GIVE US THIS DAY OUR DAILY BREAD" if I live on past experience.

I cannot say "FORGIVE US OUR TRESPASSES AS WE FORGIVE THOSE WHO TRESPASS AGAINST US" if I harbor a grudge.

I cannot say "LEAD US NOT INTO TEMPTATION" if I deliberately place myself in a position to be tempted.

I cannot say "DELIVER US FROM EVIL" if I am not prepared to fight evil with the weapon of prayer.
I cannot say "THINE IS THE KINGDOM" if I do not give the King the disciplined obedience of a loyal subject.
I cannot say "THINE IS THE POWER" if I fear what people may do to me.
I cannot say "THINE IS THE GLORY" if I am seeking glory for myself.
I cannot say "FOREVER AND EVER" if my horizon is bounded by the things of time.
—Author Unknown

Higher level

Toward the end of His ministry our Lord takes His disciples to another level in the science of prayer.

> "And I will do whatever you ask in my name, so that the Son may bring glory to the Father. You may ask me for anything in my name and I will do it" (John 14:13, 14).

> "Then the Father will give you whatever you ask in my name" (John 15:16).

> "In that day you will no longer ask me anything. I tell you the truth, our Father will give you anything you ask in my name. Until now you have not asked for anything in my name. Ask and you will receive and your joy will be complete. . . . In that day you will ask in my name" (John 16:23, 24, 31).

His name will add efficiency to our prayers. His identification with His children is so complete that their prayers are really His prayers. The Father accepts their prayers as readily as He does the prayers of His Son. The secret is in Paul's favorite expression—"In Christ." Paul's gospel maintains that the Father deals with those who are "in Christ" in the same way He does with His Son. All things "are yours, and you are of Christ, and Christ is of God" (1 Corinthians 3:23, 24).

The bank of heaven

We come to the bank of heaven with a blank check signed by Jesus Christ. There is no danger of an overdraft. The resources are unlimited. No checks are returned because of insufficient funds. The bank stands behind its promises. Jesus is our Guarantor, our Surety. All of His promises are true. He cannot fail.

We have come across something basic, elemental, even crucial. What does it mean to pray in the name of Jesus? Is it the mere repetition of that name? Once again we must ask ourselves, could this become a kind of magic? Are we to *use* that name—or rather to pray *in* that name? We must not be superficial here. It is too important.

I find this word from Ellen White very illuminating: "But to pray in Christ's name means much. It means that we are to accept His character, manifest His Spirit, and work His works"—*The Desire of Ages*, p. 668. The implication is that we are not qualified to present our prayers in His name unless and until we meet the conditions.

The first condition is to accept His character for all that it is—pure, righteous, spotless, without blemish, impeccable, and blameless (there are truly not enough adjectives to describe it). His is the only righteousness we will ever have.

The second condition is to manifest His spirit. Love, forgiveness, mercy, acceptance, gentleness, kindness, meekness, sympathy, compassion—the list is only beginning. Paul's comment is in order: "Your attitude should be the same as that of Jesus" (Philippians 2:5).

The third condition is to work His works. Healing, teaching, preaching, serving, comforting, and encouraging are a few such works of Jesus. "I tell you the truth, whatever you did for one of these least brothers of mine, you did for me" (Matthew 25:40).

It seems clear therefore, that to pray in His name is to accept Him fully, to identify with Him completely, and "to be made new in the attitude of your minds, and to put on the new self, created to be like God in true righteousness and holiness" (Ephesians 4:23, 24). To put on Christ is to adopt His lifestyle and manner. But there is something that comes before lifestyle and manner.

> "To all who received him, to those who believed in his name, he gave the right to become children of God—children born not of natural descent, nor of human decision or a husband's will, but born of God" (John 1:12, 13).

Martin Luther said it well, "Imitation does not make sons, but sons make imitators." The Master's words made a deep impression on the disciples and formed the basis for their mission. After the ascension they came together to worship in His name. Their preaching and teaching were done in that name. The name of Jesus was the subject of their conversation. New converts were baptized in His name. The sick were healed, devils cast out, and miracles wrought in Jesus' name.

> "Christ's name was to be their watchword, their badge of distinction, their bond of union, the authority for their course of action, and the source of their success. Nothing was to be recognized in His kingdom that did not bear His name and superscription"—*The Acts of the Apostles,* p. 28.

The terms of reference have not changed. His name is still "above every name" (Philippians 2:9).

Take the name of Jesus with you,
Child of sorrow and of woe;
It will joy and comfort give you
Take it then where'er you go.

Take the name of Jesus with you
As a shield from every snare
If temptations round you gather
Breathe that holy name in prayer.
—Lilian Baxter

Higher still

In John 17 this lofty concept of prayer is raised higher still. Jesus reveals to the disciples that the unity that exists within the Godhead is what He has in mind for redeemed humanity. This is higher than the human thought can reach!

> "My prayer is not for them alone. I pray also for those who will believe in me through their message, that all of them may be one, Father, just as you are in me and I am in you. May they also be in us so that the world may believe that you have sent me. I have given them the glory that you gave me, that they be one as we are one: I in them and you in me. May they be brought to complete unity to let the world know that you sent me" (John 17:20-23).

We are included in His prayers. He prays for us that our "faith may not fail" (Luke 22:31). When temptations assail us, He sets limits on the enemy so that he "dare not go one hairbreadth beyond his appointed sphere"—*Our Father Cares*, p. 59. Jesus' prayers for us are a protective shield. His prayer life is both example to us and proficiency for us. He does all this so that we may be His powerful statement to convince the world that God has sent Him.

5

The Prioritized Life

> "But seek first his kingdom and his righteousness, and all these things will be given you as well" (Matthew 6:32).

Prayer clears up the vision. We begin to see as with a wide-angle lens—and in multiple dimensions. We begin to see straight—and with unclouded vision. Our discernment is enhanced.

Christians should not be the most gullible people in town. Prayer also helps us to grow up—to mature. Prayer helps us put first things first—to prioritize. Prayer helps us distinguish between what is major and what is unimportant—and provides wisdom to know the difference. Prayer illumines our decisions and informs our judgment.

With the deepening of the prayer life comes wisdom. "Wisdom is supreme, therefore get wisdom" (Proverbs 4:7). "If any of you lacks wisdom, he should ask God, who gives generously without finding fault, and it will be given him" (James 1:5).

Christians should be the most balanced of people. There

should be a certain steadiness and good judgment about us that commends our faith to the world around us. I am sure you remember the poem we used to say in elementary school, "If you can keep your head while all around you people are losing theirs and blaming it on you . . ."

Believe me when I say that the church is in great need of insightful, well-balanced saints. It could well be our greatest need—good, sanctified judgment. One of the great Scottish preachers used to say rather bluntly, "If you have sinned, God will forgive you, if you have weaknesses of the flesh, He will give you strength, but if you are lacking common grace [sense], neither God nor the devil can help you." A bit overstated, but insightful nonetheless.

Not in the cloister

The life of prayer is not an isolated life. We live on earth amidst earth's problems and trials. We cannot say, "Stop the world—I want to get off." "My prayer is not that you take them out of the world . . ." (John 17:15). We cannot withdraw into a monastery. The Bible does say to pray without ceasing. It does not say, however, to do nothing but pray. "He who does nothing but pray will soon cease to pray, or his prayers will become a formal routine"—*Steps to Christ*, p. 101. Prayer is not the end—it is a means to the end. The early Methodists had a phrase for it—"means of grace."

Character development is what our Christian growth is all about. God wants us to develop symmetrically. There should be no flat spots, no rough edges. This is the "washing, ironing" time, Ellen White says. We cannot afford to neglect life's pressing duties. It is in the midst of these pressing duties that character is formed. Prayer prepares us to face, not escape, the nitty gritty routine of daily existence. And it is these experiences that smooth the rough edges.

"Nothing is more needed in our work than the practical results of communion with God"—*Gospel Workers*, p. 510.

A spirituality that shuns the routine is probably false. We have all heard the preacher's remark about one of his deacons who was so heavenly minded that he was of no earthly value. After commenting extensively on the Mary-Martha story, Ellen White concludes:

> "There is a wide field for the Marthas, with their active religious work. But let them first sit with Mary at the feet of Jesus. Let diligence, promptness, and energy be sanctified by the grace of Christ; then the life will be an unconquerable power for good"—*The Desire of Ages*, p. 525.

Inreach versus outreach

This brings us to the matter of inreach versus outreach—a current issue in the Adventist church. Some have made it an "either-or" matter. The focus of some is all on inreach, with total emphasis on the devotional life. Others would concentrate on outreach as if it were the all in all. Really, there is no dichotomy here. It is not either-or, it is both-and.

A praying church is a working church. The praying church has bifocal vision and grows in all dimensions—spiritually, numerically, and in wisdom and knowledge. Paul's prayer for the believers at Ephesus was that "you being rooted and established in love, may have power with all the saints, to grasp how wide and long and high and deep is the love of Christ, and to know this love that surpasses knowledge—that you may be filled to the measure of all the fullness of God" (Ephesians 3:18, 19).

Someone has written a book with the fascinating title, *The Split-level Fellowship*. The author makes the observation that too many of us live on the lower level—uninvolved, making very little spiritual progress. Behind it all is the prayer life. It is true that one can be involved in a multitude of religious activities without prayer, but no one who has a rich prayer experience can be idle. It seems then that a dynamic prayer life is the elevator to upper-level living.

The prioritized life looks like this: First God; then others; and last, self. D.L. Moody had a recipe for spiritual growth that he regularly recommended to new converts: Spend fifteen minutes a day talking to God. Spend fifteen minutes a day listening to God speak to you through His Word. Spend fifteen minutes each day talking to someone about God, and you will be a growing Christian. One of our church youth leaders said something more than forty years ago that has influenced me to this day: "This is the rule for every morning," he told a group of young people. "Talk to God before you talk to man; read what God says before you read what man says."

Prioritizing—putting first things first—is one of the great organizing principles of life. It controls our time and directs our energies. We do not fly off in all directions. People who have their lives together in this way can carry tremendous responsibilities and back-breaking work loads without burnout. They have learned to wear the world as a "loose garment." They take their work seriously, but not themselves. They are cheerful and optimistic.

I have been privileged to know some of these spiritual people (see Galatians 6:1), and my life has been enriched. They fit no socio-economic, gender, or racial mold. Life has not been for them a "crystal stair." They have had their ups and downs, their share of sorrows and disappointments. They are not necessarily church officers or ordained ministers.

What distinguishes them is their quiet dignity, a genuine God consciousness, and an unshaken confidence in the power of prayer. Through experience they have come to value the things that count. It has pleased God to place them in the churches as "those able to help others" (1 Corinthians 12:28). We should recognize their value, seek them out, and learn from their experience. They are great prayer partners and mentors. But there is one caveat. We must "test the spirits to see whether they are from God" (1 John 4:1). The saints I refer to do not trumpet their goodness.

The church that prays together grows together, works together, and joins hearts and hands together to reach out to the needy world around it. Prayer opens eyes and ears to human need. The church that walks with God refuses to be preoccupied with its own internal affairs. This is why the Holy Spirit refuses to let us settle down in contentment with our "spiritual" ghetto experience, no matter how pleasant it is. As the eagle stirs her nest, so He disturbs us. Prayer was never designed to make us comfortable. Prayer does not take the place of mission, loving "service in overalls" in the trenches.

As a denominational employee, I am sobered by Ursula Soleck's challenging poem:

What finally shall we say
At the last moment
When we will be confronted
By the unimaginable,
The One
Who could not be measured or contained
In space or time,
Who was Love
Unlimited?

What shall we answer
When the question is asked
About our undeeds
Committed
In His name—
In the name of Him
For whose sake we promised
To have courage
To abandon everything?

Shall we say

That we didn't know—
That we couldn't hear the clatter
Of hearts breaking—
Millions of them—
In lonely rooms, in alleys and prisons
And in bars?

Shall we explain
That we thought it mattered
That buildings were constructed
And maintained
In His honor—
That we were occupied
With the arrangements
Of hymns and prayers
And the proper, the responsible way
Of doing things?

Shall we tell Him
That we had to take care
Of the orderly definition of dogmas
So that there was no time
To listen to the sobbing
Of little ones
Huddled in corners,
Or the silent despair
Of those already beyond sobbing?

Or shall we say this too:
That we were afraid—
That we were keeping busy with all this
To avoid confrontation
With the reality of His meaning
Which would lead us to repentance—
That it was fear that kept us hiding
In church pews
And in important boards and committees
When He passed by?"

Ellen White's pointed words add to my discomfort, although I am sure they are good for me:

> "Pray that He [God] will give you a heart of flesh, a heart that can feel the sorrows of others, that can be touched with human woe. Pray that He will give you a heart that will not permit you to turn a deaf ear to the widow or the fatherless. Pray that you may have bowels of mercy for the poor, the infirm and oppressed. Pray that you may love justice and hate robbery, and make no difference in the bestowal of your favors, except in the cases of the needy and the unfortunate. Then the promises recorded in Isaiah 58 will be fulfilled to you"—*Welfare Ministry*, p. 84.

Powerful—penetrating!

The church that is responsive to human need will be effective in prayer. The prayers of its members will be focused, and they will then be heard. Heaven will respond. "Then you will call and the Lord will answer, you will cry for help, and he will say: 'Here I am'" (Isaiah 58:9).

It is guaranteed.

6

In Community

"Again I tell you that if two of you on earth agree on anything you ask for, it will be done for you by my Father in heaven. For where two or three come together in my name, there I am with them" (John 18:19, 20).

The church is people in community—the community of those who are "being saved" (Acts 2:47). One theologian put it this way: "The Church is Christ existing as community!"

The church is not just a group of pious people who have come together on their own to form a society of like-minded people. It is made up of men and women and boys and girls who have answered Christ's call and accepted Him as Lord and Savior. They belong to Him, and they also belong to each other. To use Paul's expression again, they are "in Christ," and thus very much bound up together.

What a fellowship! "We proclaim to you what we have seen and heard, so that you also may have fellowship with us. And our fellowship is with the Father and with his Son, Jesus Christ" (1 John 1:3, 4). Church members need each other. They pray for each other. This binds and ties them together. Not only do they pray for each other, but they pray together as often as they can.

"Pray for each other so that you may be healed" (James 5:16), the Bible says. And as we pray for each other, the church becomes a healing community. Someone has called prayer the transforming fellowship. The church that prays rightly becomes a radically transformed community. A praying Christian is an agent of change. "The prayer of a righteous man is powerful and effective" (James 5:16).

So it was in the apostle's day. "Every day they continued to meet together in the temple courts. They broke bread in their homes and ate together with glad and sincere hearts, praising God and enjoying the favor of all the people" (Acts 2:47). People called these early Christians the new people of God or the "third race." "All the believers were together and had everything in common" (Acts 2:44).

When it comes together for worship, the church is instructed specifically to pray "for everyone—for kings and all those in authority, that we may live peaceful and quiet lives" (1 Timothy 2:1, 2). We should pray for city hall, the courthouse, the governor's mansion, and the White House. We should pray for world leaders—even heads of totalitarian states. The early Christians prayed for Nero. Our prayers are not to be exclusive, narrow, and self-centered. We can say with John Wesley, "The world is my parish," and with the songwriter, "This is my Father's world."

This kind of praying has a powerful effect on those who pray and on those who hear this kind of praying. No human being is beyond the compass of God's love and concern. No one is out of His reach or out of His mind. "This is good, and pleases God our Savior, who wants all men to be saved and to come to a knowledge of the truth"

(1 Timothy 2:3). This kind of prayer focus increases the heart capacity of the church and tunes us in on heaven's wave length. It takes us out of ourselves and rids us of exclusivity.

Our brothers and sisters who live under difficult political situations need to know that the family of God worldwide is praying about these conditions. As these words are written, serious conditions threaten the cause of God in many parts of the world. It is our duty to pray for stable governments so that our brothers and sisters "may live peaceful and quiet lives" (1 Timothy 1:2).

This kind of prayer helps us say not only the right things but also wise things. Things that make for peace and unity. It may be appropriate in some instances to let government leaders know we are praying for them. God wants to give "us favor before the world until our work is done."

Healing community

The church is full of needy people. We live in a broken world, and signs of that brokenness can be seen in the community of faith. We come from all kinds of backgrounds and have been abused by the enemy. Many hide their soul hunger, while others are in the greatest need but don't know it, and still others feel shame and are driven to despair because of their sins. They need our prayers and understanding.

We carry all kinds of hostilities and resentments. Through communion with God we are made whole again. The inner civil war is over. We are ready to grow in grace and ready to grow together. The character and characteristics of Christ are to be implanted in the soul.

> "And we, who with unveiled faces all reflect the Lord's glory, are being transformed into His likeness with ever increasing glory, which comes from the Lord, who is the Spirit" (2 Corinthians 3:18).

In one oft-told story, a little girl prays, "Dear God, make all the bad people good, and all the good people nice to each other." The greatest dangers to the church are from within. Satan would like to revive those old hostilities and divisions, but as long as the community continues in prayer and in its walk with God, the enemy is held at bay. "The powers of darkness stand a poor chance against believers who love one another as Christ has loved them"—Ellen G. White, *S.D.A. Bible Commentary,* Vol. 5, p. 1141.

Let's make it practical. A brother or sister is having problems and showing symptoms of a serious spiritual sickness. What shall we do? Gossip? Wring our hands in frustration? Look the other way? "Brothers, if someone is caught in a sin, you who are spiritual should restore him gently. But watch yourself or you may be tempted" (Galatians 6:1).

Consider this not uncommon problem: Two faithful members have become estranged over some disagreement. They don't speak to each other anymore. What to do? "You who are spiritual" (praying saints), do whatever is necessary to reconcile the two. Ellen White has this to say: "His people are to possess the elements of reconciliation"—*Fundamentals of Christian Education,* p. 479. It is prayer that makes the difference—the prayers of people who love each other. We cannot afford to ignore the effect of broken relationships on the total fellowship. Bickering and strife are a hindrance to our prayers.

When we invest prayer time in our brothers and sisters, our love for them and our interest in them grows. We cannot be indifferent to their needs. We can't just pass them by as the priest and Levite passed by the poor man on the Jericho road. The opposite of love is not hatred—it is indifference. This is the indictment of Laodicea. Ellen White adds this word: "Many will allow a brother or a neighbor to struggle unaided under adverse circumstances"—*Christ's Object Lessons*, p. 383.

The selfish life is a shut-in, claustrophobic existence. The selfish person has been described as being "like a thin shaving of wood, curling up around the void of his inner nothingness." We have a duty to pray for each other. It is an absolute necessity. The greatest benefit comes to us. Prayer for others draws us out of our shells and crowds out selfishness.

I understand that the following prayer was found on the body of a soldier during the civil war:

I prayed for strength that I might achieve;
I was made weak that I might learn humbly to obey.

I asked for health that I might do greater things;
I was given infirmity that I might do better things.

I asked for riches that I might be happy;
I was given poverty that I might be wise.

I asked for power that I might have the praise of men;
I was given weakness that I might feel the need of God.

I asked for all things that I might enjoy life;
I was given life that I might enjoy all things.

I got nothing that I had asked for,
but everything that I had hoped for.

Almost despite myself my unspoken prayers were answered;
I am, among all men, most richly blessed.

There is too much bitterness, there are too many bad feelings, in the church today. Sometimes we even allow doctrinal and theological discussions or organizational issues to divide us. People take sides. The church is divided. Congregations become weak. The devil has a field day.

Let the healing process begin—God's way! "Pray for one another that you may be healed." Let us remind ourselves that praying for motes to be removed from fellow members' eyes is futile when we have beams in our own!

There are conditions to answered prayer. Growing Christians who pray for each other come to see their brothers and sisters in an altogether different light. When the inner eye is opened, and we look at "these matters without prejudice, we shall see some things to excuse, and some things to commend. and fewer to censure"—Ellen G. White, *1888 Materials,* Vol. 1, p. 106.

Forgiving spirit

Another condition is a spirit of forgiveness:

> "For if you forgive men when they sin against you, your heavenly Father will also forgive you. But if you do not forgive men their sins, your heavenly Father will not forgive your sins" (Matthew 6:14).

We cannot mistreat people and expect answers to our prayers. Peter tells husbands to treat their wives with respect, "so that nothing will hinder your prayers" (1 Peter 3:7). I have already said that Christians are change agents, but change agents must first be changed themselves. If our prayer lives are genuine, our personalities will be improved. We will be easier to live with. People will be drawn to Christ because of us, and we will have a wholesome influence in the home, the neighborhood, on the job, and in the church.

Paul said something about "the fragrance of life" (2 Corinthians 2:16). This unselfish, transformed lifestyle results in growth in grace and in "favor with God and man" (Luke 2:52).

Relationship has to be one of the most overworked words in our speech—a real buzz word. We use it without thinking. It has been trivialized in many ways. But it is hard to improve on the concept. Let's not throw out the baby with the bath water. Jesus taught us that relationships are the essence of life with God. He modeled for all to see just how these relationships should function. "Grace and truth [reality] came through Jesus Christ" (John 1:17).

The relationship that controls all other relationships, of course, is our relationship with God. This relationship enriches and enhances every other. It must be maintained and strengthened at any cost. Prayer has its covenantal aspects. We have promised to pursue His friendship and company, not fitfully and spasmodically, but faithfully and steadfastly. The Old Testament uses the expression "cleaving" to or "holding on" to God. It was said of Hezekiah that he "held fast to the Lord and did not cease to follow him" (2 Kings 18:6).

The current word is *discipleship*. Prayer therefore involves holding on to God in the manner of the Old Testament worthies. It requires constancy. The whole of life is God-oriented. The total person is involved in this relationship. Jesus expressed it as loving the Lord with heart, soul, mind, and strength. Such is the real meaning of the life of prayer.

The biblical concept of a prayer life is that it is a "walk." It is progressive. As with a friend, there is mutuality, togetherness. "Do two walk together except they have agreed to do so?" (Amos 3:3). "But if we walk in the light as he is in the light we have fellowship with one another" (1 John 1:7).

Like the horizontal and vertical holds on old TV sets, a healthy prayer life adjusts and clears up all of our relationships—vertically, between us and God, and horizontally, between us and our fellow human beings. And like the walk of faithful Enoch, the outcome is an eternity with God.

7

The Spirit Helps Us

"In the same way the Spirit helps us in our weakness. We do not know what we ought to pray for, but the Holy Spirit himself intercedes for us with groans that words cannot express" (Romans 8:26).

The Holy Spirit is anxious to help us get our prayers through. He has a special assignment—to work on us to prepare us for our walk with God. His ministry is not the same as that of Jesus the Mediator. Christ is the one who opens up the channel. He is the ladder whose base rests on the earth and from there extends all the way to the throne of God. He is the one great mediator between God and man.

The text says we do not know how to pray as we should. At best we are still little children—there is much we do not know about God and spiritual things. The Holy Spirit is well qualified to help us. He is the chief administrator of the work of God on earth. Jesus came to reveal and represent His Father. The Holy Spirit comes to represent

Jesus Christ. This is the age of the Spirit. He is our personal teacher. Jesus called Him another Counselor. "And I will ask the Father, and he will give you another Counselor to be with you forever" (John 14:16).

It is difficult to translate into our language the rich meaning of the word *paracletos*—the title Jesus gives the Holy Spirit. He is more than a Comforter, as some translations have it. His work is not restricted to that of Counselor either, as some of the newer versions put it.

We can understand a little better what Jesus had in mind by the way the word was used in His day. In everyday language, a *paracletos* was a very special friend who stood ready to help, especially in times of need or in emergencies. Soldiers applied the name to their army buddies—to the persons assigned to look after them. Sometimes it was used in a legal sense, as of a representative at court. This is the usage we find in 1 John 2:1 (Advocate).

As applied to the Holy Spirit, however, the Paracletos is everything to us on earth that Christ was when He was with His disciples. He is called "Another Counselor" (John 14:16). One Bible student calls the Holy Spirit Christ's "Alter Ego." I don't know whether this statement is too strong, but Jesus did say "He will not speak on His own; He will speak only what He hears, He will tell you what is yet to come. He will bring glory to me by taking from what is mine and making it known to you" (John 16:13, 14). One thing is clear—the Holy Spirit does not bring a separate agenda.

We are placed in the charge of the mighty Counselor, the Third Person of the Godhead, who takes care of our every need. Whatever the impediment to our prayers, whatever keeps us away from the Savior, He addresses and cares for. Jesus has put us in His hands. He shows us our sins, shows us Christ's righteousness, warns of judgment—the penalty for sin—and then makes us presentable for our walk with the King. "He saved us through the washing of rebirth and renewal by the Holy Spirit" (Titus 3:5).

What does this have to do with prayer? Everything. It is the Holy Spirit who makes Christ real to me—so real that I want to talk to Him, to reach out and touch Him, and tell Him all that concerns me. This is how Jesus can be in our midst. This is how He could say, "And surely I am with you always, to the very end of the age" (Matthew 28:20).

I am always in touch. There is no cumbersome system involving intermediaries and assistant mediators and go-betweens. Direct access—direct dial, if you please—is available. And more than that, the Holy Spirit, our Paracletos, is there to prompt us—lest we forget or become too busy—that the line is open and that Someone wants to hear from us.

The Spirit prompts our prayers. He helps us say the right things. If He did not, we would ask amiss, for all the wrong things—things that would harm us. He puts it in our hearts to pray for specific needs and people. There is such a thing as praying in the Spirit. He is our voice coach. He helps us overcome our fear and timidity. He unlooses our stammering tongues and makes us articulate—even eloquent, in the best sense of the word.

Again, He is not our Mediator in the sense that Jesus is. The Mediator pleads His blood, presents His sacrifice. The Holy Spirit works on the human instrument. We have help on both ends—a Mediator in heaven and a Counselor on earth!

As Ellen White wrote:

> "Pray that the mighty energies of the Holy Spirit, with all their quickening, recuperative, and transforming power, may fall like an electric shock on the palsy stricken soul, causing every nerve to thrill with new life, restoring the whole man from his dead, earthly, sensual state to spiritual soundness"—*Testimonies,* vol. 5, p. 267.

When we have this experience, our prayers will take on new life and vigor. Worship services will become throne-room experiences, ushering us into the very presence of God. "And God raised us up with Christ and seated us with him in the heavenly realms" (Ephesians 3:6). "A foretaste of glory divine" the hymn says. We must, then, stay on good terms with the Holy Spirit. The apostle Paul tells us that "if anyone does not have the Spirit of Christ, he does not belong to Christ" (Romans 8:9). We also know that He is "given to those who obey him" (Acts 5:32). Obedience to the dictates of the Holy Spirit is a matter of real concern. "Do not grieve the Holy Spirit of God" (Ephesians 4:30).

The Spirit makes God real to us and brings great joy and peace into our hearts. He endows the church with gifts. He produces in us the fruit that certifies the genuineness of our conversion.

> "Having believed, you were marked in him with a seal, the promised Holy Spirit, who is a deposit guaranteeing our inheritance until the redemption of those who are God's possession—to the praise of his glory" (Ephesians 1:13, 14).

When we have the Holy Spirit with us, our prayer experience will be dramatically enriched and deepened, like monotones bursting into living color, like dead taste buds coming to life. J.B. Phillips, the Bible translator, said that his experience in working with the book of Acts was at times like rewiring an old house when suddenly the power comes on. A nerve is struck—a responsive chord is touched. And then, as one of the spirituals says, "There's a little wheel a turning in my heart."

This experience is meant to be the norm; it is not reserved for "super saints." The Holy Spirit is available to every child of God.

> "For we were all baptized by the one Spirit into one body—whether Jews or Greeks, slave or free—and we were given the one Spirit to drink" (1 Corinthians 12:13).

Weak and needy though we may be, it is our privilege to enjoy the presence of the Holy Spirit at all times. In fact, we should cultivate His company. "Do not get drunk on wine, which leads to debauchery. Instead, be filled with the Spirit" (Ephesians 5:19). The inspiration that moved the "holy men of old" literally meant "God-intoxicated"—God-driven. This is the experience heaven has made available to us.

We are totally dependent on the Holy Spirit for everything that has to do with our prayer life, beginning with the new birth. "No one can see the kingdom of God unless he is born again" (John 3:3). Without the new birth, there is no spiritual life—no seeing, no hearing, no awareness, no communication.

The work of the Holy Spirit is immeasurably great. David pled with God not to "take your Holy Spirit from me" (Psalm 51:11). And the apostle Paul gives us this good advice: "Since we live by the Spirit, let us keep in step with the Spirit" (Galatians 5:25).

8

Praise

"From the rising of the sun to the place where it sets, the name of the Lord is to be praised" (Psalm 113:3).

Praise is lifting the heart heavenward in gratitude and thanksgiving, with deep feelings and appropriate words. Praise gives wings to our prayers. People who praise God mount up with wings as eagles. "The soul may ascend nearer heaven on the wings of praise"—*Steps to Christ,* p. 104.

Praise is something all created beings owe to God. It springs from the attitude of gratitude. Praise is adoration, and it is integral to prayer. Without the element of praise, prayer is not complete. Praise is worship of the highest order—it brings glory to God.

We cannot help but be impressed with the timeliness of God's special message for this generation:

"Fear God and give him glory, because the hour of his judgment has come. Worship him who

> made the heavens, the earth, the sea and the springs of waters" (Revelation 14:6, 7).

There is to be in the end time a community of loyal citizens of the kingdom of heaven who have clear and distinct views of the character of God. They witness to His creative and redemptive power. In the midst of a society of ingrates, they praise their God because they know Him and His power to save, and they believe in the ultimate triumph of His love. "I will extol the Lord at all times, his praise will always be on my lips," said David during one of the most trying periods in his life (Psalm 34:1).

The saints John speaks about so often are witnesses, and they give this witness in tough times even at the peril of their lives. Our word for witness comes from the Greek *martyr*—literally, one whose life is on the line—who is totally committed. So a martyr is one who has made the supreme witness.

Our petitions and supplications are acceptable to God. Our requests are pleasing to the Father. "By prayer and petition, with thanksgiving, present your requests to God" (Philippians 4:6). He tells us to ask. Prayer is conversation, and it takes on many forms—intercession, pleading, appeal, complaint, request, penitence, confession, and so on. But it is the life itself that gives the highest praise. "I urge you, brothers, in view of God's mercy, to offer your bodies as living sacrifices, holy and pleasing to God—this is your spiritual act of worship" (Romans 12:1).

> "Through Jesus, therefore, let us continually offer to God a sacrifice of praise—the fruit of the lips that confess his name. And do not forget to do good and share with others, for with such sacrifices God is pleased" (Hebrews 13:15).

This kind of praise brings us into "the Presence"—beyond the requests and the petitions and the asking. Envision a child running past secretaries and attendants through the doors of a corporate office. He bounds like an athlete onto the lap of the company president. "What do you want?" the CEO asks. "Nothing, Dad. I just want to be with you." The lyrics of the song say it well, "I just came to praise the Lord." Our praise is extremely pleasing in His sight—it brings glory to His name. Let's add a little more praise to our prayer life. The effect on the church and on each member will be invigorating, and it will be pleasing to God.

We praise God in our own individual way on the basis of our personal experience with Him. To put it another way, praise puts our fingerprint—our signature—on the testimony we bear. Praise is about what He has done for me. Genuine praise can never be second hand. My attitude of gratitude and my expression of praise arises naturally when I realize the ways in which God's blessings have come uniquely to me. In the words of the song, "Great is Thy faithfulness, Lord unto *me*."

As Ellen White observes:

> "Every individual has a life distinct from all others and an experience differing essentially from theirs. God desires that our praise shall ascend to Him, marked by our own individuality. These precious acknowledgments to the praise of the glory of His grace, when supported by a Christian life, have an irresistible power that works for the salvation of souls"—*The Desire of Ages,* p. 347.

Spiritual formation

We take our spiritual formation from scripture—both Old and New Testaments. Every prayer example is strong on praise. This aspect of prayer reaches its peak in the Psalms. The Psalms are songs of praise. Many of them were used for public worship. What an impressive sight it must have been—thousands of worshipers, accompanied by stringed instruments, singing with great feeling about the greatness and goodness of their God.

The hymn is a song ascribed to God—addressed to Him. The great hymns are modeled after the Psalms. They speak of His might and power. "O, God our help in ages past." "Eternal Father, strong to save." And "Majesty"—one of the newer hymns. Gospel songs—songs of experience addressed to fellow human beings—are meaningful and appropriate. But nothing can take the place of the song that speaks directly to God. "Let the word of God dwell in you richly as you teach and admonish one another with all wisdom, and as you sing psalms, hymns and spiritual songs" (Colossians 3:16).

Praise and public worship

The worship of God should be intentional—not necessarily highly structured, but carefully thought through. There is a theological, a biblical, basis for this. God demands intelligent worship. This was the burden of Jesus' conversation with the woman at the well.

> "Yet a time is coming and has now come when the true worshippers will worship the Father in spirit and truth, for they are the kind of worshippers the Father seeks" (John 4:23).

But there should always be opportunity for spontaneous expressions of praise. We should leave some room for the Holy Spirit to move. And we should prompt each other to testify. "Let the redeemed of the Lord say this . . ." (Psalm 107:2).

Toward the end of history, John sees the faithful ones overcoming Satan "by the blood of the Lamb and by the word of their testimony" (Revelation 12:11). When we speak words of praise to God, it has a powerful effect on us—a kind of reflex action. This is true in the experience of the individual Christian as well as of the corporate church. There is strength and power in the name of the Lord. The witness of such a group of worshipers is compelling. That is why "The Father is seeking these kinds of worshipers." The voice of praise confuses the enemy. It is the incense that gives the devil a headache. When we learn how to praise God "in His sanctuary," our churches will become resurrection centers.

Paul describes the kind of praise services that meet the divine approval: "But if an unbeliever or someone who does not understand comes in while everybody is prophesying, he will be convinced by all that he is a sinner and will be judged by all, and the secrets of his heart will be laid bare. So he will fall down and worship God, exclaiming, 'God is really among you'" (1 Corinthians 14:24, 25).

The worship experience of every Adventist church should be inviting. Praise should be the centerpiece of worship. People should leave our services of worship lifted up and invigorated, having sensed God's presence.

With the voice

The Battle Creek church in the 1890s wanted an organ to enhance the services. Mrs. White counseled against it. There were so many needy fields at home and abroad. She was not against organs per se, but she felt the timing was bad. (In fact, some years later, she spoke proudly of one of the churches that had purchased a building with "a fine pipe organ.") She sent a message to the believers explaining her position:

> "As you meet from Sabbath to Sabbath you need no expensive organ in order to sing praises to Him who has called you out of darkness into His marvelous light. Let the heart's adoration be given 'Unto him that loved us and washed us from our sins in His own blood.' Let the love of Christ be the burden of the minister's utterances. Let it be expressed in simple language in every song of praise. Let the inspiration of the Spirit

> of God dictate your prayers. From Sabbath to Sabbath let the song of gratitude, the fruit of the lips, ascend from the family altar, let it be heard from the pulpit, and echo through the aisles and galleries of the church. As the minister speaks to you the words of life let your heartfelt response testify that you have received the message as from heaven. . . . This response to the inspiration of the Holy Spirit will be a strength to your own souls and an encouragement to the assembled congregation. It will give some evidence that there are in God's building living stones that emit light. Will this not be more acceptable to God than the sounds you may produce from the most costly instrument of music?"—General Conference *Bulletin,* January 28, 1893.

We, too, are proud of our sister churches that have the finest of musical instruments, and I am sure God is pleased also. But we need not feel deprived if we are not so blessed in our little congregation, as long as we have voices to praise Him.

Some of the members at Battle Creek must have taken these words to heart, because I have been told by one who was there that at times there were fervent responses during the services at the old Tabernacle. There was even an occasional "hallelujah!" "This is very old fashioned I know" Mrs. White admitted, but it will be "a thank offering to God for the bread He has given to feed the hungry soul"—*Ibid.*

This is the preparation we all need in order to join with the worshipers in the throne room. In this kind of worship, the church above and the church below are already joined in spirit. Is it too much to hope that the spirit of true worship will take hold and control of every assembly of the saints? Is it possible? Is this experience reserved only for super saints and mystics? What prevents it from happening? When we are ready to receive our exalted Lord as King of our lives, He will make Himself manifest. There is no lack in Him—and no unreadiness. Mercy drops 'round us are falling. He has not forsaken us. "He's only a prayer away."

However, we must not demand a "cloud nine" experience every time we assemble. The manner in which our Lord is pleased to make Himself manifest to us cannot be programmed by the worship committee. In public worship, the family of God gathers to look to Him in praise and adoration—"our eyes are upon You." He is still in charge. All the decisions are in His hands.

One of the great stories of the Old Testament is King Jehosaphat's remarkable victory over the combined forces of Ammon, Moab, and Mount Seir. As the vast army of the enemy approached Judah's vulnerable positions, the king was encouraged by the prophet not to panic but to look to the God of Israel for deliverance. "Do not be afraid; do not be discouraged. Go out to face them tomorrow and the Lord will be with you" (2 Chronicles 20:17).

The next day the king adopted an unheard-of strategy. He appointed singers to be in the vanguard, leading the army of Judah "to praise him [the Lord] for the splendor of his holiness as they went out at the head of the army, saying: 'Give thanks to the Lord, for his love endures forever.' As they began to sing and praise, the Lord set up ambushes against the men of Ammon and Moab and Mount Seir who were invading Judah, and they were defeated" (2 Chronicles 20:21, 22).

Ellen White pictures the powers of darkness as seeking to envelop the people of God with a cloud of discouragement—to shut them off from the light of Christ's countenance.

> "I saw we must be rising and keeping the ascendancy above the powers of darkness. Our

> God is mighty. I saw singing to the glory of God often drove the enemy, and praising God would beat him back, and give us the victory"—Ellen G. White, MS. 5, 1850.

Our services of praise here should take us forward to the great praise service over there, where the heavenly and earthly branches of the family of God, finally united physically, will be joined in worship. There will be heard the call to worship:

"Praise your God, all you His servants, you who fear him both small and great!" And the thunderous response is "Hallelujah! For our Lord God Almighty reigns. Let us rejoice and be glad and give him glory!" (Revelation 19:5, 6).

There is no cloud to sadden the assembly. The causing curse is no more. All nature joins the chorus. From constellation to galaxy to island universe, there sounds forth praise, and the whole creation is filled with the sound.

9

Sharpening the Edge

"See, I will make you into a threshing sledge, new and sharp with many teeth. You will thresh the mountains and crush them, and reduce the hills to chaff (Isaiah 41:15)." "If the axe is dull and its edge unsharpened, more strength is needed but skill will bring success (Ecclesiastes 10:10)."

There is a lot of talk these days about being on the cutting edge—being out in front. This is what God has in mind for every individual Christian and every congregation. "The Lord will make you the head, not the tail. If you pay attention to the commands of the Lord your God . . . you will always be at the top, never at the bottom" (Deuteronomy 28:13).

The United States Army has a slogan: "Be all that you can be."

A church strong in mission, empowered by the Holy Spirit, and in which all the gifts are operative and the members alert and awake to every opportunity for service, is God's ultimate weapon. Greater efficiency, greater growth in grace and knowledge, greater wisdom and skill in service, is the divine mandate. The effective prayer life keeps us on the cutting edge. We ought to be out front in every category.

Addition and Multiplication

We work on the plan of addition, while God works on the plan of multiplication.

> "Grace and peace be yours in abundance [multiplied] through the knowledge of God and of Jesus Christ . . . For this reason make every effort to add to your faith goodness; and to goodness knowledge; and to knowledge, self-control, and to self-control, perseverance; and to perseverance, godliness; and to godliness, brotherly kindness; and to brotherly kindness, love. For if you possess these qualities in increasing measure, they will keep you from being ineffective and unproductive in your knowledge of our Lord Jesus Christ" (2 Peter 1:2, 5-8).

We are God's witnesses, His weapons, His instruments—links in the chain of salvation let down to this world. Yahweh calls us His threshing instrument, which He wants to keep sharp, powerful, and effective. Mechanics take special and particular care of their tools. Like the threshing machines that reap great fields of grain in a short time, His people too are to be efficient and effective in all they do. He has made every provision for us to be on the cutting edge. "His divine power has given us everything we need for life and godliness" so that we "may participate in the divine nature" (2 Peter 1:3).

Charles Spurgeon, the celebrated London preacher, watched a farmer laboriously sawing wood. He was almost dwarfed by the huge pile of logs facing him. The saw obviously needed sharpening. "Why don't you sharpen your saw, sir?" asked Spurgeon. "I don't have time," the farmer responded. It does take time and effort to keep the edge honed. "If the axe is dull and its edge unsharpened," the wise man observes, "more strength is needed, but skill will bring success" (Ecclesiastes 10:10). Our prayer experience has a sharpening effect on every aspect of life. Prayer enhances the prospect and "increases the yield."

Prayer Activates the Gifts

Church is the place where the gifts of the Spirit are polished, whetted, and activated. The prayers of the church "fan into flame the gift of God" (2 Timothy 1:6). These gifts have been poured out on the church by the God of superabundance. Says Ellen White: "Talents that are not needed are not bestowed."—*Testimonies*, vol. 9, p. 37. The church should be much in prayer that these gifts come alive and be fully operative. A gift is a terrible thing to waste.

"Now to each one the manifestation of the Spirit is given for the common good" (1 Corinthians 12:7). The endowment is unrestricted. Christ left it on deposit upon His ascension. It is inexhaustible—and it belongs to every child of God. It is a divine legacy, "not of works, lest anyone should boast" (Ephesians 2:9). Every member has been granted a portion of the endowment. Every member is in a certain sense a conduit of this revenue for the enrichment of the fellowship. This commerce, this enterprise, this bank of spiritual gifts, is also under the stewardship of the Holy Spirit. "All these are the work of one and the same Spirit, and He gives to each one just as He determines" (1 Corinthians 12:11).

Intentional Steps

We cannot leave such an important matter to chance. I am impressed by a sentence from a recent publication of the North American Division Church Ministries Department:

> "We believe that in these times, God wants each Seventh-day Adventist congregation to be strong in Christ's mission, visibly empowered by God's Holy Spirit. To achieve this vision of the congregations strong in mission and empowered by the Holy Spirit, intentional steps must be taken."—*A Shared Vision For The Local Church*, p. 4.

The key word is *intentional.* Prayer and planning go hand in hand. Goal-setting is not an unspiritual activity. Again, the NAD *Shared Vision* publication says (page 31):

> "Goal-setting in the local church is primarily the process of finding God's will for the church and its activities . . . Significant seasons of prayer are especially important during leadership retreats and annual planning councils. The foundation for any vision for mission is built on our knees."

It all begins with prayer. Martin Luther used to tell his students that to pray well is the better part of study. What would it mean to the cause of God on earth if every board meeting, committee meeting, and planning session were bathed in prayer and the agenda focused on mission—on the gifts and the development of people to fulfill their potential? Our heavenly Father has provided His church with a rich dowry. When we look at what God has provided, the favor He has shown His people, the gifts He has granted, we should be encouraged. We are in a win- win situation.

Surprises in Store

I must raise a bit of caution here. The church that goes to its knees in search of God's will is in for some surprises. This always happens when we pray, "Lord, what will You have me to do?" When the early church got "into prayer," "the place where they were meeting was shaken" (Acts 4:31). It was no longer business as usual. The status quo was gone. From then on, it was either a riot or a revolution. They could never settle on their lees. Theirs was an exciting life, but also in some respects frightening.

> "A life of monotony is not the most conducive to spiritual growth. Some can reach the highest standard of spirituality only through a change in the regular order of things. When in His providence God sees that changes are essential for the success of the character-building, He disturbs the smooth current of the life."—*Gospel Workers*, p. 269.

At times, change is uncomfortable. We get into a groove, a set pattern, and we want to stay there. But the Holy Spirit is creative. He keeps us on the cutting edge. He gives us peace of mind but never lets us be satisfied with mediocrity. "Listlessness and ineffeciency are not piety."—*Christian Service,* p. 223.

The Spirit urges us on to be all that we can be. We are Spirit driven. The times demand men and women who are innovative, who will work diligently to find new and better ways of reaching out to their communities. We need a large coalition of dynamic spiritual entrepreneurs "who can put new life into old methods of labor and can invent new plans of awakening the interest of church members and reaching the men and women of the world."—*Evangelism,* p. 105. Be ready, because this robust prayer life that we are moving into will produce visionaries and venturers "who will not carry forward the work in the lifeless way in which it has been carried forward in the past."—*Evangelism*, p. 70.

Congregations that want things to continue as they are may be shaken up when they really get into serious prayer. For one thing, spiritual gifts will come alive. Pastors will become talent scouts and coaches, discovering and activating the latent gifts that have always been there among the people of God. Then will come the surprises. Some unlikely giftbearers will come forward. This is to be expected. But we must be sure to apply the right criteria. We have a theology of ministry solidly based on Scripture. Ministry does not belong only to ordained pastors and elected officials. The commission is given to the whole church. The Lord has given to each one a work to do.

> "Not more surely is the place prepared for us in the heavenly mansions than is the special place designated on earth where we are to work for God."—*Christ's Object Lessons*, p. 327.

Those who have a rich prayer experience have the inclusive vision of the church's ministry. The entire church is to be involved in ministry.

Unemployed or Underemployed

There is the tragedy of the unemployed and also the travesty of the underemployed. There are also the unemployable. The church is the only community that has the possibility of zero unemployment. There are no unemployables in God's economy. Every God-given gift is needed to make the work a complete whole. Church leaders should spend much time in prayer for wisdom to assist each member in finding and occupying his or her place of service. The question is not whether they should serve, but where and how. What are their gifts? Church members should be equipped to serve up to the maximum capacity indicated by their gifts and experience. The church should erect no glass ceilings to prevent members from rising higher and still higher in the service of their Master. Leadership's first responsibility is to equip God's people for works of service.

Power for Service

Power in the service of Christ is not a resource in short

supply, to be grasped and held onto as if it were running out. It is unlimited, infinite, renewable, and will be given to us without measure. When we arbitrarily limit the development of church members for the ministry, we come under Ellen White's indictment of some who held responsible positions in her day:

> "The work of God is retarded by the criminal unbelief in His power to use the common people to carry forward His work successfully."
> —*Review and Herald,* July 16, 1896.

The Spirit is not bound by precedents. The gifts are not restricted by previous condition, gender, or national origin. God is an equal-opportunity Employer! Earth-shaking, pew-shaking change is inevitable. How will the church react? Adjustments will have to be made. Eli may have to listen to little Samuel! The mantle of leadership and representative ministry may be placed on our sons or our daughters. All of us will have to say, "This is the Lord's doing, and it is marvelous in our eyes!"

The church that prays well puts itself under the direct administration of the Holy Spirit. We cannot take Him for granted, nor can we restrict His sovereignty. But as we listen to Him and follow His directions, we shall become those sharp instruments "having teeth." No longer will Satan be able to take the people of God for granted, either! This is the climate, the culture, the mindset, that will keep us on the cutting edge.

Pastors are called "to train the church members . . . to seek for a deeper experience themselves, and to work for others."—*Gospel Workers*, p. 196. The two go together. The deeper experience leads us to work for others. Avery Dulles states this well:

> "But it would not be completely Church unless it went forth from its assemblies to carry on Christ's work in the world. The Church's

> existence is a continual alternation between two phases. Like systole and diastole in the movement of the heart, like inhalation and exhalation in the process of breathing, assembly and mission succeed each other in the life of the Church. Discipleship would be stunted unless it included both the centripetal phase of worship and the centrifugal phase of mission."—*Models of the Church*, p. 220.

The Holy Spirit will surely place a burden for lost humanity on our hearts when we begin to pray aright.

Planning is Spiritual

We have been using the word "intentional"—the sense of which is calculated, designed, planned, deliberate, premeditated. This planning, if it is to be approved of God, cannot be haphazard and slipshod. Every congregation in the land needs revival. Every congregation needs to get serious about renewal—to get down to business. Plans should be laid and carried out to bring about this awakening. If we are really serious, we will address the task methodically, thoughtfully, intelligently, and thoroughly, leaving no stone unturned. We need to ask ourselves some probing, even disturbing questions. We need to do this individually and as a church body. "Lord, what do You want me to do as an individual? Lord what do You want us to do as a church?"

Our Bodies a Sacrifice

The apostle Paul urges us to offer our "bodies as living sacrifices, holy and pleasing to God—this is your spiritual act of worship" (Romans 12:1). To be on the cutting edge spiritually has its physical dimension, because we are not separate parts. We are a unity—indivisible. The Bible is clear that the body and the mind—the moral and spiritual powers—are interwoven, of one fabric. The physical, the spiritual, the mental, the emotional, constitute the whole person. In finding out about prayer, we become aware of the need for discipline, and that includes the whole of life.

> "Everyone who competes in the games goes into strict training . . . therefore I do not fight like a man beating the air. No, I beat my body and make it my slave so that after I have preached to others, I myself will not be disqualified for the prize" (1 Corinthians 9:24-27).

Daniel and his companions had this winning attitude, this keen insight into the realities that kept them on the cutting edge. The narrative is crisp and insightful:

> "But Daniel resolved not to defile himself with the royal food and wine, and he asked the chief official for permission not to defile himself in this way . . . Please test your servants for ten days: Give us nothing but vegetables to eat and water to drink . . . At the end of the ten days they looked healthier and better nourished than any of the men who ate the royal food" (Daniel 1:8, 11, 15).

Church Under Conviction

Prayer brings conviction. A congregation needs to set aside blocks of time when members come together for spiritual inventory—to review the state of the church. Are we moving ahead, making progress, gaining ground? What are the vital statistics? Corporations do this all the time. We need this kind of honest evaluation, as a church and individually.

The Spirit speaks to praying churches. This is what happened at Antioch. "While they were worshipping the Lord and fasting, the Holy Spirit said . . ." (Acts 13:2). Jesus made us a promise: "But the Counselor, the Holy Spirit, whom the Father will send in my name, will teach you all things" (John 14:25).

If we want to be on the cutting edge in ministry and spiritual growth, we shall have to follow the Spirit's counsel. If we want God to hear us when we pray, we shall have to listen when He speaks. It may be that the Spirit is saying to us, Get out on the cutting edge in matters of health—those issues and concerns that have to do with your physical body. This too is "your spiritual act of worship" (Romans 12:1). The results will be positive—even dramatic.

"Every church is in need of the controlling power of the Holy Spirit," Ellen White said to the youth of her day, "and now is the time to pray for it . . . The Holy Spirit communicates with all who are doing God's service."—*Testimonies,* vol. 6, p. 267. Then she counsels these young workers:

> "Continue to work with tact and ability . . . Make regular, organized efforts to lift the church members out of the dead level in which they have been for years. Send out into the churches workers who will live the principles of health reform . . . See if the breath of life will not then come into our churches. A new element needs to be brought into the work."—*Ibid.*, p. 267.

When we follow the Spirit's counsel, Paul's words will take on a greater meaning: "Then you will be able to test and approve what God's will is—his good, pleasing, and perfect will" (Romans 12:2). We shall have clear, sharp minds, renewed strength, and vigor.

As together we work through the special instructions and counsels the Holy Spirit wants to share with the church in the end-time, the Word becomes more effective and more precious. A praying church is a tremendous support system. In unity is strength. We encourage each other, we pray for each other, and we grow together.

A People Prepared

We are talking about a people prepared, sharpened, and

ready for combat with the real problems and challenges of life. A people with a clear understanding of the issues and the times. A people aware of basic human need and possessing the skills to meet those needs. Ellen White called us a people "walled in with light." When total darkness covered Egypt for three days, "all the Israelites had light in the places where they lived" (Exodus 10:23). The prophetic portrait is of a people not only skilled in the mechanics of prayer, but actually living by every word that proceeds out of the mouth of God.

Jesus has special words to say to these people who live on the cutting edge of spiritual readiness at a time when the ultimate darkness settles in on the planet:

> "Be dressed ready for service and keep your lamps burning, like men waiting for their master to return from the wedding banquet, so that when he comes and knocks they can immediately open the door for him. It will be good for those servants whose master finds them watching when he comes" (Luke 12:35-38).

10

To the Ends of the Earth

" 'My food' said Jesus, 'is to do the will of him who sent me and to finish his work' " (John 4:34).

"Then he said to his disciples, 'The harvest is plentiful but the workers are few. Ask the Lord of the harvest, therefore, to send out workers into his harvest field' " (Matthew 9:37).

"And out of the temple came a loud voice from the throne, saying, 'It is done!' " (Revelation 16:17).

If we ever doubted that God's special message for these days could go to the ends of the earth in a short time, it must have been before the Berlin Wall came down and before the collapse of dictatorships in eastern Europe. We were all caught by surprise.

In the same manner, Ellen White says that "the final movements will be rapid ones"—*Testimonies,* vol. 9, p. 11. And these dramatic movements will be under the direct supervision of the Holy Spirit.

Global village

The world is indeed a global village. Instant communication with virtually every neighborhood, bailiwick, and barrio on Planet Earth is already possible. People in distant, isolated villages hear world news on their radios. How information reaches remote areas of the globe and grips the imagination of the multitudes is still a wonder.

The great heavyweight champion Muhammed Ali was the best-known personality of his day, bar none. Not the pope, nor the president of the United States, nor the leader of the Soviet Union, but a descendant of slaves, had the highest name recognition of any person in the world—even in the interior of the People's Republic of China! How can this be accounted for? Scholars are still writing papers about this phenomenon.

Christians are well aware of the communications skills of their God. The symbolism of angels (messengers) flying in mid-air broadcasting globally is a divine statement about God's determination to reach earth's masses with His redemptive messages. He will not permit the signals to be jammed forever. The timetable is with Him. "When I act who can reverse it?" (Isaiah 43:13).

Many years ago Mrs. White wrote an encouraging letter to her friend, Mrs. S.M.I. Henry. Mrs. Henry had been a prominent leader in the women's temperance society before becoming a Seventh-day Adventist. I am sure both women had much in common. They shared a burning desire to see the work of God go forward with greater force and threw all their energies into the cause. In anticipation of the completion of God's work on earth, Ellen White wrote with great conviction.

> "When the third angel's message shall go forth with a loud voice, and the whole earth shall be lightened with His glory, the Holy Spirit is poured out upon His people. The revenue of glory has been accumulating for this closing work of the Third Angel's Message. The prayers that have been ascending for the fulfillment of this promise, the descent of the Holy Spirit, not one has been lost. Each prayer has been accumulating, ready to overflow and pour forth a healing flood of heavenly influence and accumulated light all over the world" (Letter 98a, 1899).

The emphasis is on the mighty power of the Holy Spirit. He gives impetus to the work. He motivates and sends us out to the ends of the earth.

Our prayers our driven

It is a distinctive mark of Adventist culture to talk about the end—to anticipate the end in our day. We are a future-oriented people. We expect a sudden, cataclysmic end. We are apocalypticists of the first order. We cling to the belief that He will perform all of this in our day.

Our prayers are driven by this expectation. In the model prayer, Jesus directs us to pray that the plans and purposes of His Father shall come to fruition. "Your kingdom come." The church is a community of people bound up together in prayer for the return of Jesus.

"You ought to live holy and godly lives," Peter says, "as you look forward to the day of God and speed its coming" (2 Peter 3:12). The rabbis had a saying: "If Israel kept the law for one day, Messiah would come." The total commitment of God's people to their Creator—their absolute loyalty to Jesus Christ and His commands (see Revelation 12:14)—opens the way (and this is beyond our comprehension) for Him to set in motion the final movements.

Paul assures us that "the Lord will carry out his sentence on earth with speed and finality" (Romans 9:28). Ezekiel's vision has the angelic beings speeding back and forth "like flashes of lightning" (Ezekiel 1:14)—an indication of the blinding speed with which the purposes of God will be accomplished. There will be a consummation of all things. Christians are urged to pray for this day and to second their prayers by earnest labors.

Tapping the source

The early church tapped the Source and unleased floods of spiritual power. From their seasons of united prayer, they went forth as an invincible army. This what John reports: "I looked, and there before me was a white horse! Its rider held a bow, and he was given a crown, and he rode out a conqueror bent on conquest" (Revelation 6:2).

It is about time that the church militant put on her battle gear—the armor resplendent.

> "For our struggle is not against flesh and blood. . . . Therefore put on the full armor. . . . Take the helmet of salvation and the sword of the Spirit, which is the word of God. And pray in the Spirit on all occasions" (Ephesians 6:13-18).

In the thick of battle, communication is crucial. Prayer keeps us in contact, ears open to receive orders from headquarters. The soldiers come together to hear His voice and to hear from each other—to confirm the divine signals and strategies. There is always a divine plan of operation, but timing is of the essence. We don't want to run ahead of our Commander.

We have the experience of the early church on record: "After they prayed, the place where they were meeting was shaken. And they were all filled with the Holy Spirit and spoke the word of God boldly" (Acts 4:31). It is instructive to study the composition of their prayers.

> "Now consider their threats and enable your servants to speak your word with great boldness. Stretch out your hand to heal and perform miraculous signs and wonders through the name of your holy servant Jesus" (Acts 4:29, 30).

Their prayer was focused by global mission and the glory of God. They did not bring their little self-centered shopping lists. They had learned to pray the larger prayer.

Martin Luther once said:

> "Prayer is made vigorous by petitioning, urgent by supplication; by thanksgiving, pleasing and acceptable. Strength and acceptance combine to prevail and secure the petition"—Quoted in James Houston, *The Transforming Fellowship*, p. 259.

They went from those prayer sessions girded for battle, empowered for their extensive labors. So successful were they that Paul could say during his lifetime that the gospel "has been proclaimed to every creature under heaven" (Colossians 1:23).

"All that the apostles did, every church member today is to do"—*Testimonies*, vol. 7, p. 33.

Prevailing prayer shakes and moves us out of our complacency, our little sealed-off private worlds, and joins us together with the Christ whose great heart yearns passionately for His lost children. Prayer brings us into sympathy with our Creator, who has suffered for millennia because of sin's terrible effect on His universe.

> "Those who think of the result of hastening or hindering the gospel think of it in relation to themselves or the world. Few think of its relation to God. Few give thought to the suffering that sin has caused our Creator" —*Education*, p. 263.

Our prayer becomes more and more attuned to Jesus' petitions.

Prayer brings the atmosphere of heaven to this earth. Praying Christians are surrounded with this positive force field. We take our environment with us. The old Puritan preacher, John Brown, used to say, "It's not so much getting us into heaven as it is getting heaven into us." Before the work of God can be finished in the world, it must be finished in our hearts.

On finishing the work

We began this chapter with reference to the finishing of God's work in the earth. This "finishing of the work" that we talk about so casually is a task beyond human comprehension. As we consider it, there are at least two errors to avoid. The first is to repeat the phrase as a kind of shibboleth—some magic mantra—in a thoughtless way. This use of the phrase indicates shallowness of thought, and we certainly wouldn't want to trivialize such a serious matter. The other error is to look at the task as being impossible (according to our calculations)—to resist any consideration of our involvement in it. This leads to cynicism, doubt, and unbelief.

Both miss the mark. Both misconceptions bias our prayer lives. How can we pray for the kingdom to come if we believe it is an impossibility? And if finishing the work is a meaningless phrase, what difference does it make if we pray for the kingdom to come or not?

The intelligent believer knows something of the great challenge, but he realizes at the same time that it is also the great commission. "And this gospel of the kingdom will be preached in the whole world as a testimony to all nations, and then the end will come" (Matthew 24:14). The Savior spoke these words. Our prayers and expectations must coincide with Scripture. We do not underestimate the enemy, but we are not sent out in our own strength. We have weapons. "The weapons we fight with are not the weapons of the world. On the contrary, they have divine power to demolish strongholds" (2 Corinthians 10:4).

The Word of God is the great offensive weapon in the arsenal. It is dynamite (from the Greek word *dunamis*)—it is explosive. It has no equal. It was by this word that the universe came into being. Its power cannot be exaggerated. Prayer, however, is the lighted fuse that ignites and releases the power resident in the Word.

No one can measure the progress and extent of God's redemptive mission. We are no better informed than Elijah. He thought he was the only one still faithful! Angels belt the globe with hands linked to keep the forces of evil and destruction at bay until the mission is accomplished. "The eyes of the Lord range throughout the earth to strengthen those whose hearts are fully committed to him" (2 Chronicles 16:9). He is ever seeking—searching for the slightest indication that some heart is turning toward Him.

If we only knew the extent of His guardianship and the special care He exercises for every man, woman, and child on the planet—all 4.5 billion of us—our surprise would be greater than Elijah's. If we could only see the numberless fiery chariots strategically placed all 'round about us, in readiness for the final offensive, we would shout aloud "The battle is not ours, it is the Lord's."

We know exactly what our posture should be in this watching, waiting time. The orders are clear—watch, pray, work. We should have an intense interest in the progress of the work in every quarter of the globe, and our prayers "should go out, like sharp sickles, with the laborers in the great harvest field"—*Testimonies*, vol. 5, p. 162. The final alert calls for a mighty prayer offensive. Our prayer experience must go into overdrive. We have an understanding of the times, we know heaven's expectation for us. "God will do the work if we furnish Him the instruments"—*Testimonies*, vol. 9, p. 107.

Breakthrough

Breakthrough will come—and I am talking about the final breakthrough! In fact, it is already at hand, and long overdue. The great breakthrough awaits our "demand and reception." All heaven is restless. We can almost hear the rustling of angel's wings. They want to get on with the rest of the story. The prophetic scenario is already drawn. It is a thrilling, encouraging picture. The Lord of harvest has given us a preview of the final scenes in the drama. Here are some excerpts from the script:

> "Many. . . . will be seen hurrying hither and thither, constrained by the Spirit of God to bring the light to others. . . . The Holy Spirit is poured out upon all who will yield to its promptings, and casting off all man's machinery, his binding rules and cautious methods, they will declare the truth with the might of the Spirit's power. Multitudes will receive the faith and join the armies of the Lord. . . . By thousands of voices all over the earth, the warning will be given. . . . many whose minds were impressed have been prevented from fully comprehending the truth or from yielding obedience. . . . honest children of God sever the bands which have held them. Family connections, church relations, are powerless to stay them now. . . . Notwithstanding the agencies combined against the truth, a large number take their stand upon the Lord's side"—*Evangelism*, pp. 700, 701.

On occasion my family and I would go down to the Washington mall during the holiday season. What a sight is the giant national Christmas tree—134,500 brilliant midget bulbs! For months the workmen string wires, test circuits, set bulbs in their sockets, and get everything in order. Then comes the day for which they have made all this preparation—when the president pulls the switch in the East Room of the White House, and the current is turned on. The big tree so long in preparation bursts into glorious illumination.

This is what the Holy Spirit has been preparing the earth for since the reign of sin began. The seed sowing has been bountiful, the arguments have been given, the divine network is in place, worldwide. The Lord of harvest has His hands on the switch, ready to turn on the power. But even in the last visitation, He does not exclude us. We are commanded to "Ask the Lord for rain . . . " (Zechariah 10:1).

> "Let Christians ask in faith for the promised blessing and it will come. The outpouring of the Spirit in the days of the apostles was the former rain and glorious was the result. But the latter rain will be more abundant"—*Evangelism*, p. 701.

Pentecost will be eclipsed!

The future is now. "Seek for it, pray for it, believe for it. We must have it, and Heaven is waiting to bestow it. . . . Let Christians ask in faith. . . . and it will come"—*Ibid.*